CARIBBEAN

Pompidou the parrot, at Horned Dorset Primavera,
Rincón, Puerto Rico.

FROMMER'S

BED AND BREAKFAST GUIDES

CARIBBEAN

BY LUCY POSHEK

Photographed by Lucy Poshek

DESIGNED AND PRODUCED BY
ROBERT R. REID AND TERRY BERGER

MACMILLAN • USA

Frontispiece: The Copper & Lumber Store Hotel,
English Harbour, Antigua.

*The Robert Reid Associates listed as a Bed and Breakfast
Agency are totally unrelated to and independent of the
Robert Reid Associates who are the producers of this book.*

Published by Macmillan Travel
A Prentice Hall Macmillan Company
15 Columbus Circle
New York, NY 10023

MACMILLAN is a registered trademark of Macmillan, Inc.

Library of Congress Card No. 94-78856
ISBN 0-02-860063-0

A Robert Reid Associates production
Typeset in Bodoni Book by Monotype Composition Company,
Baltimore
Produced by Mandarin Offset, Hong Kong
Printed in Hong Kong

1 2 3 4 5 6 7 8 9 10

CONTENTS

GRAND CAYMAN ISLAND

JAMAICA

Caribbean

Atlantic Ocean

Sea

ANGUILLA

ST. MARTIN/ST. MAARTEN

VIRGIN GORDA
ST. JOHN

ST. BARTS

ST. THOMAS

ST. KITTS

PUERTO
RICO

NEVIS

ST. CROIX

SABA

ST. EUSTATIUS

ANTIGUA

MONTSERRAT

GUADELOUPE

DOMINICA

MARTINIQUE

ST. LUCIA

ST. VINCENT

BARBADOS

BEQUIA

MUSTIQUE

ARUBA

GRENADA

BONAIRE

CURAÇAO

TOBAGO

TRINIDAD

Crane Beach in the Barbados, one of the grandest beaches in the Caribbean, for which the Crane Beach Hotel is named.

AUTHOR'S NOTE

A Caribbean bed and breakfast isn't always easy to identify. In this guide, for instance, you will find establishments ranging from guest houses to inns to small resorts spread throughout thirty-two different Caribbean islands—each island with its own nationality and distinct heritage. The accommodations range from Bohemian to ultra-deluxe. Not only are the innkeepers from every country imaginable, but so are the guests.

Because of the rich cultural diversity of each island, you simply won't find the same types of B&B's that you are accustomed to. In place of the typical quaint Victorian, for instance, you might encounter anything from a simple, tin-roofed guest house to a seventeenth-century plantation inn to a modern, exclusive resort. The overly-decorated American bedroom has been replaced by a West Indian style of simplicity, with greater focus on the natural beauty outdoors.

Whereas breakfast has grown into the main event at most European and American B&B's, you'll find the morning meal somewhat less sophisticated in the Caribbean. With a few notable exceptions, scrambled eggs, toast, and fresh tropical fruit are about as fussy as things get down there. Besides, you may find yourself more distracted by the presence of a peacock, monkey, or yellow-feathered bananaquit at your breakfast table. The soft-as-flour sand between your toes, the sound of the croaking tree frogs, and the balmy, frangipani scented air somehow take precedence over any cravings for stuffed French toast.

In the Caribbean, no one's in a hurry. Your hosts, whether they are Spanish, British, Pennsylvanian, or island-born, will be the first to remind you that too much activity is bad for the vacationing soul.

The inns and guest houses of the Caribbean are the closest they have to true B&B's. But be forewarned that some West Indian-style guest houses, while most affordable and local in character, are not always up to American standards. The décor and amenities are basic; hot water and air conditioning might be in short supply. The inns generally offer more comfortable, charming, historically colorful accommodations. In fact, many of the inns listed in this guide are, without question, the most splendid establishments in the Caribbean. And you will soon discover that some of the finest inns are not anywhere close to a pretty beach.

On islands where there were virtually no B&B's, like Curaçao and Anguilla, small hotels and resorts were selected instead. But, like the inns and guest houses, they all share a sense of intimacy, character and personal warmth that you wouldn't find at larger establishments. Many are family-owned or managed by caring hosts who give their guests an exceptional amount of personal attention.

Today, adventurous travelers are looking for a vacation experience that goes beyond the one-port-a-day cruise or the all-inclusive, huge resort. They're discovering that intimate hotels and inns will provide a far richer experience—a chance to unwind and get a closer look at the real Caribbean.

Interior of an oceanfront villa.

Windsurfing is popular, with the instruction starting out on dry land before progressing to the water.

CINNAMON REEF

Romantic privacy

Situated on a calm, white-sand cove of Anguilla, this family-run resort manages to provide both unpretentious luxury and romantic privacy without sacrificing personal attention. Everyone seems happy here, and it's no wonder: Cinnamon Reef is the kind of place you start thinking about coming back to before you've even left.

The individual, Mediterranean-style villas offer a lavish amount of space, with multiple archways and windows, red tile floors, and thick wood beams across the high ceilings. On each balcony is a hammock where you can enjoy your welcome cocktail. Other thoughtful extras include evening hors d'oeuvres, turn-down service, twice-daily maid service, fresh-squeezed orange juice with your complimentary breakfast, room refrigerators, and hair dryers. Afternoon tea accompanied by classical music is served in the open-air lobby of the main building which overlooks Little Harbour. And

Left above, the ocean from a villa patio. Below, the beach, showing the inn and guest villas on the right, overlooking the water.

whereas most Caribbean resorts rent their water sports equipment by the hour, Cinnamon Reef includes free use of all its windsurfers, snorkeling gear, sunfish, and paddle boats.

All of this generous pampering is typical of owner Richard Hauser, who recently moved to Anguilla with his family to personally oversee the hotel he built in 1983. You'll often find Richard and his wife Carol at the bar socializing with guests during happy hour. "You can be as degenerate as you want on your private patio," he says, "but if you want to meet people, come to our bar."

Life here revolves lazily around the water, from which there is a view of nearby St. Martin. The reef-protected harbor is a perfect place for beginners to learn windsurfing, and Malt, the hotel's instructor, is topnotch.

CINNAMON REEF, Little Harbour, Anguilla, British West Indies; (809) 497-2727; Fax (809) 497-3727; Richard Hauser, owner. Represented by IHR at (800) 346-7084. Closed September 5 to October 30. Twenty-two suites, all with private baths. No air conditioning. High season rates: $250 to $350; low season: $150 to $225, including continental breakfast and all water sports. Children over 10 welcome in high season; smoking allowed; Visa/ MasterCard/American Express. Thirty-three spectacular beaches available on Anguilla. Award-winning Palm Court Restaurant (on premises), Koal Keel, and Hibernia recommended for dining.

DIRECTIONS: five miles from airport ($10 by taxi). Government requests guests to take taxis to and from airport. Car rentals available from the hotel.

COCCOLOBA HOTEL

A picture-perfect white sand beach

The sunny beaches of Anguilla (which rhymes with "vanilla") are world class, and Coccoloba Hotel overlooks a most spectacular one. A stunning crescent of powdery white sand and impossibly clear water, Barnes Bay will quite simply take your breath away.

This picture-perfect beach is rimmed by a low headland covered with sea grape (Coccoloba is Latin for "sea grape"), frangipani, and flamboyant trees. Staggered along the bluff are individual villas painted a pale yellow with white gingerbread trim. Each villa has its own patio, cathedral ceilings, and a modified split-level bedroom which overlooks a sitting area.

Coccoloba's main building—perched on the promontory with exaggerated West Indian-style cathedral ceilings—houses the reception area, restaurant, bar, tea room, and swimming pool. From the promontory lookout points you can see up the coast to yet another incredible beach, Meads Bay.

The amenities here are abundant—a welcome fruit and cheese plate, complimentary refreshments in your room refrigerator (including a free bottle of rum), a full American breakfast buffet (or continental breakfast in your room), English high tea, evening turndown service, complimentary mail service, room safes, walking canes, umbrellas, and thick terry robes.

Coccoloba was recently taken over by an Italian company, so you'll experience a Mediterranean touch here with lots of lively Italian dialogue between the staff and guests. Every Monday evening the guests are invited to a complimentary cocktail party followed by a West Indian style buffet.

The sensational beach at Barnes Bay.

COCCOLOBA HOTEL, P.O. Box 332, Barnes Bay, Anguilla, British West Indies; (800) 982-7729; (809) 497-6871; Fax (809) 497-6332; Rafael Oliveros Russian, manager. Closed September 14 to October 7. Fifty-one rooms, villas and suites, all with private baths and air conditioning. High season rates: $375 to $575; low season: $225 to $380, including full breakfast buffet. Children under 2 free; children ages 2 to 11 are $50 extra per day; smoking allowed; Italian, German and Spanish spoken; Visa/MasterCard/American Express. Complimentary water sports. Day ferries to nearby St. Martin available from Anguilla. Pavilion Restaurant (on premises) and Mango's (a short walk down the beach) recommended for dining.

DIRECTIONS: on the western side of Anguilla, between Barnes Bay and Meads Bay. Twenty minutes from airport ($15 by taxi).

Left above, guest villas. Below, a view of Barnes Bay, the beach, and the villas that overlook it all.

An ocean villa interior.

The second-floor landing.

THE COPPER & LUMBER STORE HOTEL

A swashbuckling haven for sailors

Back in the swashbuckling days of Horatio Nelson, the premier British naval base of the West Indies was at English Harbour, Antigua. It was at this time, in 1783, that the discovery of copper as a method of bottoming ships brought about the building of the Copper and Lumber Store. Situated in what would later become known as Nelson's Dockyard, the store thrived until it lost its military and commercial importance in the late nineteenth century.

During the 1980s the neglected brick building was restored and converted into an elegant, Georgian-style inn. Steeped in rich naval history, Nelson's Dockyard is now a historic national park while The Copper & Lumber Store Hotel serves as a popular gathering place for the international sailors and yachtsmen who anchor here. In the evenings you'll hear them swapping island stories in the adjoining pub and atmospheric hotel bar. Owner

The Victory Suite bedroom.

Left, the courtyard of the original building of the Copper and Lumber Store.

Alan Jeyes, a Scotsman and former sailor himself, often presides behind the bar.

The second-story guest rooms, each named after Lord Nelson's ships or admirals, are built around an arched brick courtyard. The four Georgian suites—Africa, Victory, Royal Sovereign, and Britannia—are most magnificent. Authentically detailed down to the pewter candlesticks, they boast Chippendale and Queen Anne furnishings, paned windows, seafaring prints, and Persian carpets over wood floors. Rustic stairs lead to a sleeping loft where the bed, romantically veiled in a gauzy netting, sits under the beamed ceilings. The bathrooms are paneled in warm Honduras mahogany, with slate showers and wash basins of Argentinean brass.

The raw, weathered brickwork and rough-hewn beams that have been faithfully restored throughout the hotel create an old world ambience not found at any of the beach resorts on Antigua.

THE COPPER & LUMBER STORE HOTEL, Nelson's Dockyard, English Harbour, Antigua, West Indies; (809) 460-1058; Fax (809) 460-1529; Alan Jeyes, manager. Represented by Caribbean Inns at (800) 633-7411. Open all year. Fourteen suites, all with private baths and kitchenettes. No air conditioning. High season rates: $195 to $325; low season: $85 to $165, with breakfast available for $5 to $12; MAP $40 per person. Children welcome; smoking allowed; French spoken; Visa/MasterCard/American Express. Many historic sites within walking distance. Dive and sail programs available. Beach accessed by five-minute ferry ride. Wardroom restaurant and Mainbrace Pub on premises.

DIRECTIONS: in Nelson's Dockyard, on the south side of Antigua, 30 minutes from airport ($21 by taxi).

The Victory Suite living room.

Right, Nelson's Dockyard, still a sailors' anchorage.

The rough-hewn 18th-century building.

Pondering the mysteries of the universe in the solitude of the private dock.

THE VISTALMAR

Ocean breezes and air conditioning

The Vistalmar is one of the most affordable and intimate places to stay on Aruba. Though it lacks any of the island's famous beaches, guests enjoy some uncommon amenities and individual attention they wouldn't otherwise have at a package beach resort.

Set across from the water in a reidential area next to the airport, The Vistalmar is comprised of eight one-bedroom apartments in two identical buildings. Each apartment has a similar layout, with a sea-view balcony or courtyard, living room, complete kitchen, and bedroom. Though not overly stylish, the apartments are comfortable and spacious. While refreshing ocean breezes blow steadily through the living rooms, the bedrooms are cooled by air conditioning.

Alby and Katy Yarzagaray have added many personal touches that make The Vistalmar more

Left, the inn's tropical setting.

than just your average apartment stay. Katy greets you with informal, Midwestern-style hospitality (that is, if her dogs, Hoover and Snooks, don't beat her to it). Your kitchen is stocked with welcome breakfast provisions, refreshments, and other treats that she sometimes bakes herself. Along with all the comforts of home are fresh flowers, common laundry facilities, and bicycles. And, for the grand total of $70 a day you can have the apartment and a car (which you'll need here anyway).

Both Alby, who was born on Aruba, and Katy, who has lived here since the 1960s, know all the most delightful spots on Aruba. They try to connect the individual interests of their guests with the island's offerings. Alby has built a private little dock across the street, and from here you can watch the boats drift by. But for swimming, the beaches north and south of Oranjestad just can't be beat.

THE VISTALMAR, Bucutiweg 28, Aruba, Dutch Caribbean; (011) 2978-28579; Fax (011) 2978-22200; Alby and Katy Yarzagaray, owners. Eight one-bedroom apartments and one four-bedroom villa, all with private baths and air conditioning. High season rates: $600 to $630 per week; low season: $320 to $350 per week, including welcome breakfast provisions. Car packages available. Children welcome; smoking allowed; Dutch and Spanish spoken; no credit cards. Many beaches (Manchebo is particularly stunning), shopping in Oranjestad, and casinos nearby. Mi Cushina recommended for dining.

DIRECTIONS: south of Oranjestad, very close to airport. ($7 by taxi). Car can be arranged upon check-in.

An apartment bedroom.

The sitting room of an oceanfront suite.

TREASURE BEACH HOTEL

Planters punch— the house specialty

Treasure Beach Hotel has long been a favorite choice of guests looking for a small, comfortable, extremely friendly hotel on Barbados. Situated on an idyllic, white sand stretch of St. James Beach, in Payne's Bay, this English-owned hotel enjoys a family-like camaraderie that draws its guests back again and again. In fact, more than eighty-five percent of the mostly-British guests are repeat clientele.

After staying here just one night, it's easy to see why. Two stories of suites are interconnected around a swimming pool in a cozy horseshoe shape, open to the flowery tropical garden and ocean, yet cleverly angled for maximum privacy from one another. Decorated in tropical pastels and framed batik prints, each tastefully-appointed suite is divided in half, with an air conditioned bedroom inside and a shady sitting room outside. The sitting area is like an open-air living room, complete with comfortable couches, paperback books, and a kitchenette. From

Left above, the pool and courtyard. Below, St. James Beach, immediately in front of the hotel.

here, you can socialize with other guests during the day and then close off the area with accordion-like shutters at night.

A giant mahogany tree stretches its limbs over a grassy knoll bordering the beach, pleasantly framing the view of the emerald-blue water and providing shade for sunbathers. Though all kinds of water sports—waterskiing, catamarans, windsurfers, inner tubes, and even pirate ships—are busy in the bay, the guests of Treasure Beach seem content just to relax and settle into a lounge chair with their books and tropical drinks. After your welcome Planters punch (a humdinger house specialty), the most activity you'll desire here is a bit of lazy snorkeling or a cooling dip in the pool.

Treasure Beach Hotel is one of the most hospitable and unpretentiously luxurious places you'll find on Barbados.

TREASURE BEACH HOTEL, Payne's Bay, St. James, Barbados; (809) 432-1346; Fax (809) 432-1094; John Moreton, owner; Trevor Ramsay, manager. Represented by Robert Reid Associates at (800) 223-6510. Open all year. Twenty-five suites, all with private baths and air conditioning. High season rates: $275 to $460; low season: $140 to $215; MAP supplement $45 per person per day. Children allowed on request; smoking permitted; Spanish spoken; Visa/MasterCard/American Express. Complimentary snorkeling gear. Water sports, golf, and tennis nearby. Treasure Beach Restaurant (on premises), Carambola, La Maison, and La Cage Aux Folles recommended for dining.

DIRECTIONS: on the west side of Barbados, 45 minutes from the airport ($20 by taxi). Car rental recommended.

CRANE BEACH HOTEL

Perhaps the finest beach in the world

Considered for centuries as one of the finest beaches in the world, Crane Beach boasts soft-as-flour pink sand and crystal clear waves that massage you like a gentle whirlpool. Coral stone steps lead up to the historic Crane Beach Hotel, which overlooks this lovely cove from its rugged clifftop promontory.

The Crane Beach Hotel dates back to the late 1700s when it was a private mansion of gray-white coral known as the Marine Villa. Even then, the island's plantation owners and merchants were attracted by the cool breezes and exceptional sea bathing of southeastern Barbados. In 1886, a civil engineer enlarged the mansion and opened Crane Beach as the first resort in Barbados. For over a century it was considered the premier honeymoon destination of Barbados.

Whereas the newer additions to the hotel (such as the lobby) look somewhat out-of-kilter with the

Left, the trip down the pathway to Crane Beach is well rewarded, as the stunning view of the beach on page 8 reveals.

The old 19th-century wing.

old, the original mansion is well preserved and comprises fourteen suites in the east section of the hotel. The suites are quite spacious and atmospheric, with pine floors, high ceilings, coral stone walls, canopied beds, and Hepplewhite furnishings. Tall mahogany shutters open to the startlingly blue sea, allowing the invigorating Atlantic breezes to cool the rooms. Most of the suites feature balconies (some very large) and kitchens as well.

The hotel's Panoramic Restaurant, which overlooks Crane Beach, draws many sightseers for lunch to feast on the view and local Bajan food. (Try the flying fish—a Bajan specialty.) Connecting the restaurant and hotel is a beautiful, Roman-style swimming pool with classic white columns. The blue-and-white theme of the hotel is positively dazzling under the bright Barbados sun.

CRANE BEACH HOTEL, Crane Beach, St. Philip, Barbados, West Indies; (809) 423-6220; Fax (809) 423-5343; Paul Doyle, owner; Edwin Luke, manager. Represented by Robert Reid Associates at (800) 223-6510. Open all year. Nineteen rooms and suites, all with private baths. No air conditioning. High season rates: $160 to $295; low season: $100 to $175, with breakfast available for $5 to $10 extra. AP, MAP, and honeymoon packages available. Children welcome; smoking allowed; all credit cards accepted. Top windsurfing spots nearby. Panoramic Restaurant on premises.

DIRECTIONS: on the southeast side of Barbados, about 5 miles from the airport ($11 by taxi). Car rental recommended.

Overleaf, the hotel and pool—an architect's delight.

The living room of Suite 10 in the old wing.

Owners Margit and Lars Abrahamsson enjoy their beautifully constructed bar.

FRIENDSHIP BAY HOTEL

The perfect unspoiled island

This small resort hotel is owned and run by a friendly, barefoot Swedish couple who have set a most casual tone for their guests. "My family and I have tried to create a familiar and relaxed ambience," says Lars Abrahamsson. A former sea captain, he and his restaurateur wife, Margit, searched the Caribbean for the perfect, unspoiled island and settled several years ago on Bequia (pronounced "Beck-wee") several years ago. They are still slowly upgrading the twelve-acre hotel, which was in a state of disrepair when they took it over. Though most of their guests are European, Friendship Bay is beginning to draw more Americans and even some celebrities as of late.

The smallish guest rooms are contained in several one-story buildings that rim Friendship Bay. They are simply furnished in cheerful yellow and white, further brightened by a bit of blue Scandinavian trim and vases of freshly-cut flowers. Each room

Left above, the terrace overlooking Friendship Bay. Below, the hotel pier and dive boat.

has its own stone terrace facing the bay. The reception area, breakfast room, and additional cottages are terraced up the hill. Their breakfast menu might include fresh mango, pancakes, bacon, and eggs.

But Friendship Bay is best known for its Polynesian-style beach bar and informal, adjoining restaurant. Guests can sip their welcome rum punches from unusual swinging chairs which dangle around the bar. During high season, their Saturday night "jump-ups," or dances, bring out the liveliest in islanders and guests alike.

Located nine miles off St. Vincent (called the "mainland" here), Bequia has an old-fashioned innocence not found on many islands nowadays. "You could stay on Bequia for two weeks and never run out of things to do," says Lars. "Even though it's a small island, everything is available here."

FRIENDSHIP BAY HOTEL, Box 9, Bequia, St. Vincent, The Grenadines; (809) 458-3222; Fax (809) 458-3840; Lars and Margit Abrahamsson, owners. Closed September. Twenty-seven rooms and one suite, all with private baths. No air conditioning. High season rates: $125 to $175; low season: $90 to $125, including full American breakfast. Children welcome; smoking allowed; German and Swedish spoken; Visa/MasterCard. Windsurfing, snorkeling, tennis, boat jetty, and dive programs on premises. Sailing trips through the Grenadines available. Friendship Bay Restaurant (on premises) and Gingerbread Restaurant recommended for dining.

DIRECTIONS: three miles from the airport. Car rental recommended unless you're an avid hiker.

Guest rooms are in the stone house.

Owners Sonja and Otmar Schaedle.

THE OLD FORT

A reconstructed stone fortress

The Old Fort is perched like a medieval castle on one of the highest hilltops of Bequia, commanding a panoramic view of the Grenadines. This inspired creation is the realization of a dream for Otmar and Sonja Schaedle, the inn's charming, Bavarian-born owners.

The Schaedles reconstructed their stone estate as accurately as possible over the remains of a two hundred-year-old foundation. Otmar's former profession as a history teacher gave him a fine eye for authentic detail—stone towers, arched doorways, rustic hinges, and stone walls—without any sacrifice of comfort. Though the overall impression is medieval, The Old Fort maintains an auberge kind of elegance. A typical day is spent lounging in the shady garden, listening to classical music and sharing stimulating conversation.

The tower guest rooms are large and atmospheric, with thick stone walls and floors, wonderful views

Left above, the restaurant at night. Below, the thick stone walls don't deter nighttime marauders, hence the traditional mosquito netting.

from the arched windows, and beds surrounded by mosquito netting.

While Otmar runs the inn, Sonja oversees the restaurant, which turns into a magical setting at night with its Afghan wall hangings, crackling fireplace, and profusion of candles. The delicious Mediterranean-Creole cuisine places an emphasis on fresh local fish. (Try the smoked red snapper.) Breakfasts are a delightful blend of the tropics and Europe—fresh pineapple, a salad of smoked fish, tomatoes and feta cheese, followed by eggs, bacon, and pumpernickel bread.

This Shangri-La environment is enhanced by a menagerie of gentle resident pets—dogs, cats, donkeys, peacocks, sheep, goats, lambs, and rabbits. In the morning you might be awakened by the braying of Boxi, the donkey, or the mating call of Pasha, the peacock.

THE OLD FORT, Bequia, Mt. Pleasant, St. Vincent & Grenadines, West Indies; (809) 458-3440; Fax (809) 458-3824; Otmar Schaedle, proprietor. Open all year. Six rooms, all with private baths. No air conditioning. High season rates: $80 to $120; low season: $65 to $100, with breakfast available for $10 extra; MAP plan available. Children welcome; smoking allowed but not encouraged; German, French and Italian spoken; Visa/MasterCard. Nature trails and unspoiled beaches within walking distance. Restaurant on premises; Plantation House also recommended for dining.

DIRECTIONS: ten-minute winding drive (or a very steep, 20-minute walk) to Port Elizabeth and ferry dock; about 25 minutes from the airport.

The back courtyard.

Decorated tables in the courtyard.

THE BLUE IGUANA

Lots of Bohemian island color

Nestled in a quiet nook of Bonaire's quaint capital, this unique guest house is in a historic home owned by Antillean-born innkeeper Laurie Dovale. The Blue Iguana has what Laurie calls a "barefoot ambience"—a youthful Bohemian quality which may not appeal to everyone—but you'll assuredly find more island color here than anywhere in the Caribbean.

In fact, the entire house is overflowing with color, from the thick, mustard-yellow walls and aquamarine trim to Laurie's boggling display of quirky memorabilia—salt and pepper shakers, Madonnas, plastic iguanas, dolls, and old Life magazines, to name a few. An exotic scent of sandlewood pervades the numerous common rooms which are filled with brightly painted island antiques. Laurie's collectibles are amusingly eclectic yet artfully arranged, creating the overall effect of a 1950s Curaçaoan thrift shop.

While one could spend hours just absorbing everything, guests are eventually drawn out to the covered patio which overlooks a backyard filled with

Left, above, the colorful inn building. Below, owner Laurie Dovale.

yet more rustic treasures. After a hearty breakfast on the patio you can lie in a hammock under a calabash tree and observe the passing fauna, which might include an occasional iguana, a wild *prikichi* parrot, or Laurie's pet turtle George.

The Blue Iguana is for those who want a memorable, authentic island experience. Its guest rooms are simple and comforts basic, appealing more to free spirits than luxury-seekers. And, unlike the larger, more isolated hotels north of town, the Blue Iguana is right in Kralendijk. All of four blocks long, its picturesque, Dutch-style shops and cafés are just a short stroll away.

THE BLUE IGUANA, Kaya Prinses Marie #6, Kralendijk, Bonaire, Netherlands Antilles; (011) 5997-6855; Fax (011) 5997-6855; Laurie Dovale, owner. Open all year. Seven rooms share two baths. No air conditioning. High season rates: $65 to $80; low season: $50 to $65, including full breakfast. No children; smoking limited; Spanish, Dutch, Papiamentu, and some Italian spoken; no credit cards. Personal island tours and bike rentals available. Diving, snorkeling, and downtown Kralendijk nearby. Bistro Des Amis, Sonny's Place, and Den Laman recommended for dining.

DIRECTIONS: in the heart of Kralendijk ($8 to $10 by taxi). One-day car or motorbike rental recommended for exploring the island.

The front of the inn seen from the street.

Owner Ditta Balstra.

LEEWARD INN GUEST HOUSE

Reef diving is a must here

The Leeward Inn is a simple, no-frills guest house that is most memorable for its delightful innkeepers, Don and Ditta Balstra. Their sense of *bon bini* (which means "welcome" in the local Papiamentu language) embodies much of what makes Bonaire such a harmonious island.

Their cozy café, which offers fresh, inexpensive meals, draws many friendly residents, making it easy for guests to meet local Bonaireans. The little adjoining bar is a popular hangout where you'll often find Ditta smiling and bustling around, making introductions and chatting in Papiamentu. (You'd never guess that Ditta and Don moved here from Syracuse, New York, just a few years ago.) Now and then a musician will stroll in, pick up one of the guitars, and start an impromptu concert.

Though the tidy guests rooms are very basic, painted in pale shades of green, yellow and blue, the café walls are brightened by pretty murals of Bonairean scenes and life-size renderings of locals painted by Dutch artist and café regular, Jan Bouwman. He has also added a whimsical trompe l'oeil window to the one guest room which has no windows.

As Bonaire has some of the best reef diving in the world, an underwater excursion is a must.

Left, a life-size mural in the bar.

Adjoining the back patio area of the Leeward Inn is a full service dive center where guests can arrange for lessons or certification. For those who simply want a nice beach and casual snorkeling, the dive center can also provide the half-mile water taxi to Klein Bonaire, a small, uninhabited island with incredible marine life. You can be dropped off on a deserted beach for a few hours and snorkel to your heart's content. It's *hopi, hopi bon* (very, very good).

LEEWARD INN GUEST HOUSE, Kaya Grandi 60, Kralendijk, Bonaire, Netherlands Antilles; (011) 5997-5516; Fax (011) 5997-5517; Don and Ditta Balstra, owners. Represented by Great Southern Travel & Adventures at (800) 748-8733. Open all year. Five rooms, all with private baths. Air conditioning available in one room. Year-round rates: $45 to $63, with breakfast available for $3 to $8 extra. Children welcome; smoking allowed; Spanish, French, Papiamentu, and Dutch spoken; Visa/MasterCard/American Express. Dive shop on premises. Flamingo Sanctuary, Washington Slagbaai National Park, and world class diving nearby. Harthouse Cafe (on premises), Otello's, Raffles, and Sonny's Place recommended for dining.

DIRECTIONS: three blocks north of downtown Kralendijk ($8 to $9 by taxi). One-day car or motorbike rental recommended for touring the island.

Room 4 is acutally a suite.

HOTEL PORTO PASEO

Small and intimate

Though the Pòrto Paseo is more of a hotel than a traditional bed and breakfast, it is by far the smallest and most intimate accommodation on the island of Curaçao. It's also conveniently situated right in the colorful Dutch town of Willemstad.

Originally the island's first hospital, the colonial-style hotel overlooks the St. Anna Bay and famous Queen Emma floating bridge (which swings open more than thirty times a day). Lining the waterfront across the bay are the pastel, gabled facades of Willemstad that are so reminiscent of Holland. From the open-air bar and restaurant of the Porto Paseo, you can also see the floating market—a multi-colored collection of boats that sell fresh fish and produce every morning. All of this is just a short walk or ferry ride away.

The guest rooms are modern and pristine, with high ceilings and a somewhat stark décor. They're grouped randomly over the meandering, palm tree-studded grounds in numerous yellow buildings topped with white trim and orange tile roofs, which makes a cheerful sight against the powder blue sky. Along the pathways are nearly a dozen bird cages containing cockatiels and Amazon parrots with such "exotic" names as Pebbles and Bam Bam. Parrots are also painted on the tentlike roof of the restaurant and bar where the generous buffet breakfast is served.

The Porto Paseo has its own dive center on the premises. Lessons usually start out in the swimming pool, which is enhanced by a small, artificial

Left, above, Willemstad, on St. Anna Bay, looks European. Below, diving instruction is given in the pool.

The hotel and grounds.

waterfall. Next door is a small, two-story casino where you can try your hand at blackjack and roulette.

HOTEL & CASINO PORTO PASEO, De Rouvilleweg 47, Willemstad, Curaçao, Netherlands Antilles; (011) 5999-627878; Fax (011) 5999-627969; Richard Tollafield, owner. Open all year. Forty-five rooms, one suite, and two apartments, all with private baths and air conditioning. Year-round rates: $95, including continental plus buffet breakfast. Children welcome; smoking allowed; Spanish and Dutch spoken; Visa/MasterCard/American Express. Casino next door. Historic Willemstad and many architecturally significant buildings within walking distance. Several restaurants nearby.

DIRECTIONS: in the Otrabanda district of Willemstad, about 15 minutes from the airport ($12 by taxi).

The Casino is right next door.

The lobby.

Another part of the Penny Farthing bar.

Guest room with guest.

REIGATE HALL HOTEL

Lush, tropical splendor

Once part of a citrus estate known as Reigate Hall, this Dominican hotel sits high on a mountainside amid lush, tropical splendor at the end of a winding, mazelike road above the capital city of Roseau. Thick vegetation and exotic flowers wrap around the hotel like a protective, soundproof cloak.

Built of grey flagstone and wood, the hotel looks like a cross between a modest European chalet and a ship, with its rustic stone, darkwood beams, and double A-frame roof over the restaurant and bar. Indeed, the driveway is actually lined with the thick chain from a ship's anchor, and the restaurant is uniquely hung from the second floor by these chains.

Each of the simple, comfortable guest rooms have little balconies, air conditioning, phones, and televisions. A welcome fruit basket contains paw paw, mangos, tomatoes, and limes. The high ceilings, darkwood furnishings, wooden shutters and floors add to the chalet feel.

The "hanging" restuarant is lit by numerous *Left above, the pool and guest quarters. Below, the Penny Farthing Bar.*

skylights during the day and candles at night. Traditional island specialties include such Creole delicacies as crab back, plantain, and kalaloo (a soup made from dasheen leaves). Below the restaurant is an attractive, bicycle-themed bar. A swimming pool and tennis court are also on the premises.

The rest of Dominica (which rhymes with "unique-uh") is as every bit as lush as Reigate Hall. This is one of most verdant, primeval islands in the Caribbean and a naturalist's paradise. The hotel can arange for personally guided hiking tours to many of the island's treasures, such as the Boiling Lake or Emerald Pool. If guests wish for a change from mountain scenery, they can also enjoy the nearby beachside amenities of Reigate Hall's new sister hotel, the Reigate Waterfront Hotel.

REIGATE HALL HOTEL, Reigate, Roseau, Commonwealth of Dominica, West Indies; (809) 448-4031; Fax (809) 448-4034; Reginald Shillingsford, owner. Represented by Jan Milbyer at (305) 462-0830. Open all year. Sixteen rooms and suites, all with private baths and air conditioning. Year-round rates: $75 to $95, including continental breakfast. Discounts offered for longer stays. Children welcome; smoking allowed; French and Creole spoken; Visa/MasterCard/American Express. Personal island tours available through hotel. Wednesday night barbecue and live entertainment offered at Reigate Waterfront Hotel. Restaurant on premises. The Orchard and Pearl's Cuisine also recommended for dining.

DIRECTIONS: located one mile from Roseau and 3 miles from Canefield Airport. Shuttle to and from Canefield Airport can be arranged through hotel.

The living room of a suite.

Seven Mile Beach one block away.

INDIES SUITES

A scuba diving paradise

If Grand Cayman is your destination and diving is your dream, there is probably no better place to stay than at the Indies Suites. Not only does this all-suites hotel have one of the most sophisticated scuba diving facilities on the island, but it is family-run and far more personal than the larger hotels.

Located one block from Grand Cayman's famous Seven Mile Beach, this hotel consists of forty suites arranged around a tropically landscaped courtyard, Jacuzzi, cabana bar, and swimming pool that is custom-designed for dive instruction. Decorated in pastel tones of salmon and green, the rattan-furnished suites are large, immaculate and quiet, with all the modern amenities of an apartment.

Owner Ronnie Foster, whose family has lived on the Cayman Islands since the 1700s (their grandfather built the first hotel on Cayman Brac), believes in providing lots of *lagniappes* (the Cajun word for "little extra somethings") for his guests. Among the *lagniappes* found here are complimentary

breakfasts, a lending library, welcome cocktails, individual barbecue grills and storage lockers for diving gear, plus complimentary sunset cruises, barbecue nights, and happy hours with live music

The Indies Divers program offers a wide range of packages, including beginning courses, open water certification (which can be completed in five days), PADI advanced diver instruction, and excursions on their 38-foot luxury dive boat to such world-famous diving sites as the North Wall, Devil's Grotto, Eden Rock, and unforgettable Sting Ray City, where you can feed and pet the stingrays. Among the specialty courses available are night diving, underwater photography, deep dives, and naturalist dives.

INDIES SUITES, P.O. Box 2070, Grand Cayman, British West Indies; (800) 654-3130; (809) 947-5025; Fax (809) 947-5024; Ronald Foster, owner. Open all year. Forty Suites, all with private baths and air conditioning. Five suites offer handicapped facilities. High season rates: $240; low season: $160, including continental breakfast. Children under 12 free; non-smoking suites available; Spanish spoken; Visa/MasterCard/American Express. Diving, windsurfing, honeymoon, and car packages available. Deep-sea fishing trips can also be arranged. Sting Ray City, Hell, and Cayman Turtle Farm nearby. The Wharf, The Lobster Pot, Hemingways, and The Champion House recommended for dining.

DIRECTIONS: five miles north of Georgetown, one block from Seven Mile Beach. Car rental recommended, as taxis are expensive (about $17 from the airport).

Left above, a striking birds-eye view of the inn. Below, a guest's view of the courtyard.

Scuba diving off the inn's boat "Georgetown."

SECRET HARBOUR RESORT

Mediterranean-style harbor views

Situated in the exclusive L'Anse aux Epines district of southern Grenada (pronounced "Grah-NAY-dah"), Secret Harbour is quietly removed from the big resort hotels of Grand Anse. Twenty villa-like suites, each named after one of Grenada's spices, are terraced steeply up the hill above gorgeous Mt. Hartman Bay, known as a haven for yachtsmen.

The Mediterranean design of these suites is filled with romantic details. Each wood balcony has railings carved into the shapes of lyres. Beyond the arched entry is a second set of interior brick archways that separate the bedroom from the sitting area. Antique four-poster beds, their chenille spreads decorated with red hibiscus blossoms, contrast with white rock walls and heavy beamed ceilings. The windows are also unusual, with paned, stained-glass shutters in the bedroom and a wagonwheel-shaped window over the tub. While soaking in your romantic, Italian-tiled, tub-for-two, you can observe all the sparkling boats in the harbor.

A collage of blue and orange is found throughout the hotel. The nautical blue cushions of the suite sitting areas are set atop orange brickwork. Outside are orange tile rooftops against the deep blue sky and water. Even the tilework of the attractive reception building and restaurant is cast in oranges and blues.

Poised at the edge of the steeply terraced hill is a striking swimming pool. Above this is a reception area, open-air restaurant, and bar, its tables placed to take full advantage of the peaceful view. Among the games found in the bar area is an oversized chess set carved from wood.

A guest enjoying one of the decorative bathrooms.

SECRET HARBOUR RESORT, P.O. Box 11, St. George's, Grenada, West Indies; (800) 334-2435; (809) 444-4439; Fax (809) 444-4819; Owned by The Moorings, a yacht-charter company. Open all year. Twenty suites, all with private baths and air conditioning. High season rates: $225; low season: $135 to $155, with breakfast available for $8 to $14 extra. Children under 12 not accepted; smoking allowed; German, Italian, and Spanish spoken; Visa/MasterCard/American Express. Complimentary water sports, small beach, and tennis on premises. Fishing, scuba diving, boat trips to Hog Island or Calivigny, skippered yacht trips, and island tours available. Secret Harbour Hotel Restaurant, La Dolce Vita, The Red Crab, and The Aquarium recommended for dining.

DIRECTIONS: four miles south of the airport ($10 by taxi), and 5 miles south of St. George's. Car rental not recommended.

Left, the Pimento Suite overlooks Mt. Hartman Bay.

The Bay Leaf Suite, with its beautiful four-poster beds.

The pool and restaurant.

RELAIS DU MOULIN

The look and feel of Provence

Le Relais Du Moulin (*moulin* means "mill") is dominated by a well-preserved windmill that rises from a low, pastoral hill near Sainte-Anne on Guadeloupe. Built in 1843, the windmill was used for crushing sugar cane up until 1920. Though it now houses the hotel's reception area, you can still climb its circular stairway for a panoramic view of the surrounding countryside, nearby ocean, and the isle of Marie Galante in the distance.

Fanning down the hill from here are the guest quarters, which consist of large, red-roofed bungalows with private patios. The bungalows, each divided into two units, are named after different Caribbean islands. Most units feature an airy downstairs living room and kitchenette with a spiral staircase leading to the second-floor bedroom loft. Though the hotel was built in 1979, the pale green décor, linoleum floors, and sharp angles of the interior have more of a 50s look. Many tall, louvered

Left, the old windmill now houses the reception office.

windows open up the living room to the colorful grounds.

The landscaped pathways that wind among the bungalows are abloom with multi-colored hibiscus and bougainvillea. In your walk about the grounds you may encounter goats, chickens, cats, and dogs, which adds to the pastoral effect. Next to the windmill are a restaurant, bar, and inviting swimming pool. There are also tennis courts and play facilities for children, including a long slide that dumps into a small plunge pool.

Twin beds, bidets, and a mostly French-speaking staff are just a few of the Gallic details you'll find at Le Relais Du Moulin. Except for the tropical weather (and the mosquitos—bring insect repellent), the surrounding countryside looks like it's imported straight from Provence.

RELAIS DU MOULIN, Helleux, Sainte Anne, Guadeloupe, French West Indies; (011) 590-882396; Fax (011) 590-880392; J.P. Marie, owner. Represented by ITR at (212) 251-1800. Open all year. Forty cottage suites, all with private bath and air conditioning. High season rates: $136 to $169; low season: $93 to $127, including continental breakfast. Children free; smoking allowed; French (and very little English) spoken; Visa/MasterCard/American Express. Half-mile dirt road to white sand beach. Pointe des Châteaux recommended for sightseeing. Relais Du Moulin, Les Châteaux, Le Zagaya, and La Tasana recommended for dining.

DIRECTIONS: between Sainte Anne and St. François, about 20 minutes east of the airport. Hotel can arrange transportation upon request, but a car rental is recommended.

Sitting room and patio of a guest cottage.

HAMAK

A casual air of understated elegance

In 1979 Hamak received worldwide attention as the site of the Western summit, which included President Giscard d'Estaing, President Carter, and other heads of state. This quiet resort still draws those seeking discreet privacy and seclusion. Hamak is very French but not stuffy, with a gracious staff and casual air of understated elegance.

A collection of simple, one-story bungalows are scattered randomly over five acres of flowery grounds. Some look upon the gardens while others face the phosphorescent green sea. Tall palm trees, white umbrellas on a downy-soft sand beach, and bronzed, topless French sunbathers make this one of the quintessential Caribbean beach settings. The hotel's restaurant and open-air bar take full advantage of this idyllic scene.

Furnished in teak and teal blue, the somewhat narrow bungalows are cut in half by a low divider (which also serves as a desk), with a small sitting area to one side and a bed on the other. There are two patios—one in front with a hammock, table and chairs, plus an enclosed rear patio which also has an outdoor shower. Mini-refrigerators, telephones, private safes, hair dryers, a welcome fruit basket, and complimentary beach bag are standard fare in each room. Each bungalow has a quiet, private feel,

Left above, the guest cottages are right on the beach. Below, the manicured beach.

enhanced by the carefully groomed foliage. From your patio hammock or the private beach you can survey the passing windsurfers, sunfishes, and catamarans in the calm, reef-protected lagoon.

Those who can rouse themselves out of their *hamak* will find the little French town of St. François full of lively beachside cafés and pâtisseries. Guadeloupe, the Emerald Isle, is well known for its gastronomy, with fresh food flown in daily from Paris.

HAMAK, 97118 Saint-François, Guadeloupe, French West Indies; (011) 590-885999; Fax (011) 590-884192; J.F. Rozan, manager. Represented by Caribbean Inns at (800) 633-7411. Closed August 26 to October. Fifty-six rooms, all with private baths and air conditioning. High season rates: $270 to $350; low season: $170 to $250, including full breakfast. Children welcome; smoking allowed; French spoken; Visa/MasterCard/American Express. All water sports and tennis on premises; Robert Trent Jones golf course across the street. Many restaurants nearby.

DIRECTIONS: in St. François, 40 minutes east of the airport. Car rental recommended.

A cottage's outdoor shower in use.

One of the guest suites.

JAMAICA INN

An elegant alternative to modern resorts

This exquisite, colonial-style inn is a far more intimate alternative to the modern, all-inclusive resorts that are so prevalent on Jamaica. Since it opened in the 1950s, its timeless elegance has drawn the likes of Winston Churchill, Ian Fleming, and Errol Flynn.

Situated in an exclusive neighborhood several miles east of Ocho Rios, the forty-five rooms and suites of this inn are built in a U-shape around a private, reef-protected beach and swimming pool. Thatched-roof umbrellas sit invitingly on a beach of golden sand. Overlooking this tranquil scene is an open-air dining room, cozy library, and English gentlemen's-style pub.

The guest rooms are a visual delight, painted in inviting periwinkle blue with white colonial trim and shutters. In addition to the gracefully-appointed sleeping area, each room is highlighted by a living room-sized, open-air terrace that is comfortably furnished with a sofa, wing chair and ottoman, an

Left, it's worth the trip just to have breakfast al fresco with this breathtaking view.

antique writing desk, fine lamps and prints.

The most requested guest rooms are in the west wing right over the clear, blue-green sea. From these balustraded terraces you can almost touch the colorful fish through the water. The White Suite, at the end of the wing, is utterly grand, with a huge living room opening to a waterfront balcony, a sun terrace with private swimming pool, and a private rocky promontory complete with meditative chairs.

For over thirty years the Jamaica Inn has been owned by the same family. Peter and Eric Morrow, who grew up at the Jamaica Inn, are now the second generation of resident owners. They have upheld a civilized, traditional ambience where guests still dress for dinner, and the staff—most of whom have been with the hotel for a quarter century or more—provide an old-world kind of gracious service that is rarely encountered nowadays.

JAMAICA INN, P.O. Box 1, Main Street, Ocho Rios, Jamaica; (809) 974-2514; Fax (809) 974-2449; Peter and Eric Morrow, owners. Represented by Ray Morrow Associates at (800) 243-9420. Open all year. Forty-two rooms and three suites, all with private baths and air conditioning. High season rates: $340 to $475, including full American plan; low season: $170 to $225, including modified American plan. Inquire about packages. No children under 14; smoking allowed; German, French, and Spanish spoken; Visa/MasterCard/American Express. Complimentary snorkeling gear. Plantation tours, Dunn's River Falls, rafting, Firefly (Noel Coward's home), golf, and tennis nearby. Jamaica Inn, Evita's, and The Restaurant at Harmony Hall recommended for dining.

DIRECTIONS: one-and-a-half hours east of Montego Bay Airport. Private taxi transfers available for $80 each way.

Pine Pillar, a two-story guest cottage built on a pillar of stone.

A cottage guest room.

TENSING PEN

Nature on the rocks

Tensing Pen is for those who want a back-to-nature experience—complete with Polynesian-style cottages, lush surroundings, and dramatic ocean setting—without roughing it too much.

Set at the edge of a rocky sea cliff, Tensing Pen consists of twelve thatched-roof cottages separated by meandering paths of dense foliage. Some cottages are elevated on ten-foot-high wooden pillars, creating a romantic treehouse effect. The bedrooms are octagonal-shaped, with four-poster beds and lacy linens adding a bit of refinement to the otherwise rustic décor. Double doors open from each bedroom to a patio or balcony.

The jungle-like botanical gardens have been kept as natural as possible. All the winding paths lead to various capes on the cliff's edge, which overlooks a narrow rocky cove. A rather precarious-looking bridge spans across the cove, providing a dramatic, fifteen-foot diving spot for swimmers and snorkelers.

Bathing suits and bare feet set the tone here. Guests can be as private as they want, but if anyone

Left, the inn meanders over the cliffs and rocks.

wants a bit of friendly conversation, there's usually someone lounging around in the thatched-roof, open-air communal area, where a serve-yourself breakfast is put out each morning. Aside from a few games, books and snorkeling, not much else is on the agenda. "There's very little energy here," boasts British owner Richard Murray, who first opened Tensing Pen in 1975. "People say they never felt so relaxed in their lives."

This casual, carefree place fits perfectly in Negril, a Jamaican beach resort that is notorious for its free-spirited goings-on. From Tensing Pen you can walk to numerous cafés or rustic road stands to "lime" (hang out) and "whine" (dance sensually) to the accompaniment of thunderous Jamaican music. In Negril, anything goes, and everything is "irie" (fine).

TENSING PEN, P.O. Box 13, Negril, Jamaica; (809) 957-4417; Fax (809) 957-4417; David & Bernice Cunningham, managers. Open all year. Twelve cottages and one three-bedroom house with kitchen, all with private baths. No air conditioning. High season rates: $100 to $175; low season: $70 to $125, including self-serve continental breakfast. Children welcome; smoking allowed; French spoken; Visa/MasterCard. Seven-mile beach nearby. Scuba, snorkeling, and island tours available. Lighthouse Inn, Café Au Lait, and Xtabi recommended for dining.

DIRECTIONS: in Negril, about 50 miles southwest of Montego Bay Airport. Shuttle can be arranged by hotel or at the airport ($20 to $60).

Owners Wayne and Jan MacKinnon.

MONTEGO BAY'S PREMIER GUEST HOUSE

Jamaica's friendliest hosts

This reasonably priced guest house is run by two of the friendliest hosts on Jamaica. Wayne MacKinnon, who is originally from Canada, and his wife Janet, who was Jamaican born and raised, operate this lively, sociable place with their two small boys in residence. Both of them formerly conducted tour excursions for the Sandals Resort.

Set above the Canadian consulate in the heart of Montego Bay, this Jamaican-style house features a large veranda, high ceilings in an airy living room, and cool, tiled floors throughout. Haitian and Jamaican art decorate the walls, along with large arrangements of tropical flowers and island collectibles. Off the living room are three modestly-furnished guest rooms, each with long, wicker tables for storing luggage.

Left above, the front of the house. Below, the dining room.

The atmosphere is free and easy here, with reggae music often playing all afternoon. Though it's not a fancy place, this is a perfect way to get close to the real Jamaica. Janet, whose mother is Irish and father is sixth-generation Jamaican, has a most melodic accent. She and Wayne spend a lot of time with their guests, providing fascinating details about every aspect of the island's culture.

Breakfast is served on the veranda, which overlooks Montego Bay across the street. For high-spirited guests, Janet will cook a typical Jamaican breakfast of liver and boiled green bananas, or salt fish, fried dumplings, and ackee (a cooked tree vegetable). For dinner, The MacKinnons might send you next door to the Pork Pit, an informal local place with picnic tables where you can feast on Jamaican jerk pork or chicken.

MONTEGO BAY'S PREMIER GUEST HOUSE, 29 Gloucester Avenue, Montego Bay, Jamaica; (809) 952-3121; Fax (809) 979-3176; Wayne and Janet MacKinnon, owners. Open all year. Three rooms, all with private baths and air conditioning. High season rates: $60 to $75; low season: $50 to $60, including breakfast. Children welcome; smoking permitted on veranda; French, Spanish and Italian spoken; Visa/MasterCard. Golf courses, sugar plantations, Doctor's Cave Beach, and art galleries nearby. Celico's, Pork Pit, Townhouse, and Marguerite's recommended for dining.

DIRECTIONS: in the center of Montego Bay, five minutes from the airport. Airport transfers free if booking a week or more.

PLANTATION LEYRITZ

Atmospheric stone buildings

Although the Plantation Leyritz is too large to qualify as an intimate bed and breakfast inn, it is worth a visit even if only for the day. Located in the banana plantation-covered hills of northern Martinique, Leyritz is a whole complex of atmospheric stone buildings dating back to the eighteenth century. Originally a sugar plantation, the compound was built around 1700 by Bordeaux-born Michel de Leyritz.

While some of the buildings, such as the old sugar refinery, rum distillery and master's mansion, have been turned into museums or restaurants, other historic structures have been converted into guest quarters. Also found here is an unusual museum of elaborately-costumed figurines, handmade entirely from natural plants by artist Will Fenton. All of this is spread over twenty acres of parklike grounds.

The guest accommodations are divided into four widely-varying categories. *Les Dépendances* are the most requested. Set quietly up the hill next to the restored master's mansion (which is open to the public), these old stone cottages feature traditional

Left, the restored Master's House.

A guest house that was formerly part of the slave quarters.

Creole furnishings such as canopied, four-poster beds and private balconies that look over the countryside to the distant sea. Also popular are the individual bungalows, some of which were former slaves quarters and others which are brand new.

HOTEL PLANTATION LEYRITZ, 97218 Basse-Pointe, Martinique; (011) 596-785392; Fax (011) 596-789244; Gilles Michel, reservations manager. Open all year. Sixty-seven rooms and cottages, all with private baths and air conditioning. High season rates: $130 to $140; low season: $70 to $75, including continental breakfast. Children welcome; smoking allowed; French and Spanish spoken; Visa accepted. Evening cultural programs, including June jazz festivals, are held on the premises. Nearest beach is thirty minutes away. Pool and tennis courts on grounds. Restaurant on premises.

DIRECTIONS: one hour north of the airport, just before Basse-Pointe. Car rental recommended.

The grounds, showing the former slave quarters and pool.

The Library.

HABITATION LAGRANGE

A living Caribbean romance novel

Habitation Lagrange is one of the most gorgeously bucolic hideaways in the Caribbean. With its fili-greed trim and wraparound verandas, the main mansion—once part of a sugar and rum plantation—springs straight from the pages of a Caribbean romance novel. Three other lovely annexes—two of which are pink with white gingerbread trim—are built around a big, circular swimming pool.

And *what* a setting. The inn is surrounded by magnificent gardens of huge bamboo trees and Tarzan-like vines, with a profusion of exotic birds and oversized flowers. Beyond, the lush valley seems to stretch forever with banana trees, looking like an ethereal scene from "Paradise Lost." In the mornings, the cloud-covered mountains add to the dreamy enchantment.

The French-Caribbean-style guest chambers are beautifully appointed in rich fabrics, antiques, and wicker furnishings. Acajou, a two-bedroom suite on the second floor of the mansion, commands the most outstanding view. The interior is stunningly decorated in crisp Wedgewood blue and white, with French canopied beds, polished wood floors, and brass lamps. In the bathroom is a wood-paneled bathtub, private water closet, and two pedestal sinks. Among other luxurious details found in the rooms are bold arrangements of tropical flowers, period prints, old-fashioned fixtures, and white monogrammed bed linens.

Left above, The guest quarters, left, and the main house, right. Below, the pool and breakfast terrace with the guest quarters behind.

The two-bedroom Acajou Suite.

On the main level of the mansion is an airy, mural-painted dining room with high, arched mahogany doorways. Adjoining this is a wood-paneled bar and small library. Breakfast, served on an open-air terrace, is artfully presented. Freshly sliced tropical fruits are arranged on a long tray adorned with flowers and delectable toppings such as creamy fresh yogurt and shredded coconut. *Café* is served in big French-style cups. Then you have a choice of eggs and a basket of French *pâtisseries*, such as *pain au chocolat*, croissants, and sliced baguettes.

This is your chance to practice those French verbs you learned in school, as very little English is spoken here. Habitation Lagrange is a haven for Francophiles who prefer a refined country setting to the beach.

HABITATION LAGRANGE, 97225 Le Marigot, Martinique; (011) 596-536060; Fax (011) 596-535058; Jean-Louis de Lucy, owner. Represented by Caribbean Inns at (800) 633-7411. Closed September 1 to October 15. Eleven rooms and one suite, all with private baths and air conditioning. High season rates: $300 to $375; low season: $200 to $300, including full breakfast. Children welcome; smoking allowed; French (and very little English) spoken; Visa/MasterCard/American Express. Tennis and swimming pool available. Gourmet, very expensive Créole restaurant on premises.

DIRECTIONS: thirty minutes north of the airport, just north of Marigot. Car rental recommended.

Overleaf, the dining room, with its dominating mural.

Owners Charles and Yveline De Lucy.

The De Lucys are most gracious hosts, and their lively conversations, enhanced by charming French accents, are worth the stay alone. They are quite attentive to their guests, spending time with them over breakfast and offering sightseeing tips. They will most certainly send you over to nearby l'Habitation Clément for a rum tour, or to St. Pierre, the once-thriving, turn-of-the-century town which was destroyed entirely by the eruption of Mt. Pelée.

FREGATE BLEUE HOTEL, 97240 Le François, Martinique, French West Indies; (011) 596-545466; Fax (011) 596-547848; Yveline De Lucy, owner. Represented by Caribbean Inns at (800) 633-7411. Open all year. Seven rooms, all with private baths and air conditioning. High season rates: $170 to $225; low season: $100 to $140, including continental breakfast. Children under 8 free; smoking allowed; French and English spoken; Visa/MasterCard/American Express. Good central location for touring Martinique. La Riviera, La Plantation, and Poi de Virginie recommended for dining.

DIRECTIONS: thirty minutes north of the airport, just beyond Le François. Car rental recommended.

FREGATE BLEUE HOTEL

Aristocratic hosts

This small, gingerbread-trimmed inn is run by two of the most fascinating hosts on Martinique—Yveline and Charles De Lucy. Descended from one of the first aristocratic families of the French West Indies (known as *békés*), the De Lucy name has been recognized throughout the island since the seventeenth century. It was the De Lucys who first created the Hotel Plantation Leyritz and played host to such dignitaries as President Ford and Giscard d'Estaing. And it was their cousin, Jean-Louis De Lucy, who restored Habitation Lagrange.

After selling the Plantation Leyritz, the De Lucys settled into a smaller inn on a peaceful residential hillside just outside of Le François. While they live on the first level of the main building, the second level contains a cheery breakfast terrace and guest rooms. Each cathedral-ceilinged room is spruced up by handsome family antiques such as four-poster beds, armoires, and Persian rugs. A small kitchenette is hidden in every closet. Sliding glass doors lead out to private balconies that peek through the trees to the sea and its cluster of *petite* islands. A separate guest cottage sits out by the swimming pool and its shady arbor. Water spills over the pool in a fountain-like effect.

Left, the inn and pool.

The Magnolia Room.

The well-maintained grounds provide a perfect setting for the Victorian building.

ST. AUBIN HOTEL

Victorian gingerbread for budget travelers

The St. Aubin Hotel is a perfect choice for budget travelers on Martinique. Though the Victorian mansion—built over a colonial plantation site—is a bit frayed around the edges, there is a sweetly inviting quality in its three stories of pink and white gingerbread trim. Situated five miles north of Trinité, the hotel sits high on a quiet, green hillside that sweeps down to the Atlantic Ocean.

Foret Guy, the very hospitable manager who has owned the St. Aubin for fifteen years, offers modest

Left, view of plantation fields and ocean from the second-floor balcony.

but spotless guest rooms just like those you would find at a modern budget hotel in France, with functional twin beds, square pillows, deep tubs, and hand-held shower nozzles. The second-floor bedrooms open out to a wide cement veranda which has a wonderful view of the rolling, palm-dotted hills and Ile St. Aubin, a little island off the coast. On the first floor is a pretty, wicker-filled lounge, another wraparound porch, and a small dining room where breakfast and dinner are served. The complimentary breakfast is typically French, with café au lait and buttered baguettes.

A wide expanse of lawn, ornate brickwork, and wrought-iron gates wrap around the front of the hotel. To the side is a swimming pool and garden. The St. Aubin Hotel makes a good base for driving tours to the plantations and rum factories of northern Martinique.

ST. AUBIN HOTEL, Box Postal 52, 97220 Trinité, Martinique, French West Indies; (011) 596-693477; Fax (011) 596-694114; Represented by ITR at (212) 251-1800. Foret Guy, owner. Open all year. Fifteen rooms, all with private baths and air conditioning. High season rates: $68 to $112; low season: $55 to $89, including continental breakfast. Children welcome; no smoking in dining room; French spoken; Visa/MasterCard/American Express. Pool and dining room (for guests only) on premises.

DIRECTIONS: five miles north of Trinité, 22 miles north of the airport (about $40 by taxi). Car rental recommended.

The main building.

Typical interior of a "rondavel."

VUE POINTE HOTEL

Where the island's élite meet

Often referred to as "the way the Caribbean used to be," Montserrat is still so unspoiled that its largest hotel—the twenty-eight-room Vue Pointe— would be considered small on most other islands. Nonetheless, this friendly, family-run resort is *the* social spot for tourists and islanders alike.

At the top of a hillside overlooking the verdant coastline is the main lodge, with its restaurant, swimming pool, and bar. Here you might find the Montserratian minister of culture or tourist board rep catching up on island news and gossip. At the base of the slope is a gray sand beach, an abbreviated eighteen-hole golf course, tennis courts, and popular beach bar called the Nest.

Guest accommodations at Vue Pointe are in rondavels—individual, hexagonal cottages that run down the gentle slope. Each rondavel is painted a pastel color, with lots of interesting angles inside. The rattan-filled interiors are cheerful and simply decorated, with sitting areas adjoining the bedrooms and louvered windows providing breezy cross-venti-lation.

Built in the 1960s, the Vue Pointe Hotel is owned and operated by Carol and Cedrick Osborne. Their son, Michael, grew up at the hotel and now manages

Left above, the pool and guest "rondavel" cottages over-look the bay. Below, the gray sand of the hotel beach.

it when not at college. The Osborne Family has a reputation for taking exceptionally good care of their guests. Newcomers are treated to a welcome cocktail, and every Monday evening, guests are invited to the family house for cocktails. Their Wednesday night West Indian barbecues are an island event. The huge buffet, which includes such Montserratian specialties as "mountain chicken" (frogs legs), is held around the pool to the accompaniment of a steel drum band. Among the other roster of activities is an "iguana feeding," where guests can observe wild iguanas gathering for their daily meal in a neighbor's yard.

VUE POINTE HOTEL, P.O. Box 65, Old Towne, Montserrat, West Indies; (809) 491-5210; Fax (809) 491-4813; Carol A. Osborne, owner. Open all year. Twenty-eight cottage suites, all with private baths. No air conditioning. High season rates: $159 to $175; low season: $89 to $114, including continental breakfast. Children under 12 free; smoking allowed; Visa/MasterCard/ American Express. Golf, tennis, shuffleboard, and water sports on premises. Monserrat National Museum, Fort St. George, Galway's Plantation, Galway's Soufrière, Foxes Bay Bird Sanctu- ary, and Chance's Peak nearby. Emerald Cafe, Belham Valley, and Ziggy's recommended for dining.

DIRECTIONS: on the west side of Montserrat, 4 miles north of Plymouth, 16 miles from the airport. Hotel can arrange a taxi pick- up (about $15), car rental, and free shuttles into Plymouth.

PROVIDENCE ESTATE HOUSE

On a hillside high above the sea

Providence Estate House is a delightful B&B situated on a secluded, ten-acre hillside high above the sea. The lush mountains of Montserrat form a dramatic backdrop to this tastefully-designed estate home. A luxuriant lawn and ornamental gardens spill steeply down from the inn.

Though Providence Estate was once part of a turn-of-the-century cotton mill, the original home was destroyed during Hurricane Hugo in 1989. Owner Tony Glaser, a British psychologist, and his Haitian wife, Marlene, rebuilt the house into a fresh, West-Indian-style inn—all white, with pink-trimmed shutters, and red tin roof—and it looks even better than before.

While the Glasers now reside in the U.S., Jim & Bev Harris, a wonderfully engaging couple from Maine, run the inn and live on the second level. Guests have use of the entire main floor, where a Southwest-style common room, two bedrooms, a swimming pool, and outdoor kitchenette are found.

The spotless bedrooms feature low beamed ceilings, white walls, English floral spreads, simple furnishings, and extra nice bathrooms. Each bedroom has a second access from the pool area. Thick walls cool the entire ground floor, and everything looks very new and fresh.

Jim & Bev's hospitality is much mentioned by guests, and it's no wonder. They really bend over backwards to make newcomers feel at home. Need to send a fax? No problem. Looking for a good snorkeling beach? Jim might drive you there himself. Happy hour might find you up on Jim & Bev's veranda enjoying cocktails. In the morning Jim will offer you a breakfast selection of eggs or West Indian-style oatmeal (made with cinnamon, allspice, and almonds), a soursop fruit smoothie, homemade breads, and mango or papaya.

PROVIDENCE ESTATE HOUSE, St. Peter's Village, Montserrat, West Indies; (809) 491-6476; Fax (809) 491-8476; Anthony & Marlene Glaser, owners; Jim & Bev Harris, managers. Open all year. Two rooms, both with private baths. No air conditioning. High season rates: $55 to $85; low season: $45 to $80, including full breakfast. Children welcome; smoking allowed outside only; Visa/MasterCard. Pool on premises. Black sand beach, snorkeling, bicycling, golf, and tennis available nearby. Hilltop Restaurant, Vue Pointe Hotel, and Ziggy's recommended for dining.

DIRECTIONS: near St. Peter's, on the northwest side of Monserrat, about 25 minutes from the airport ($13 by taxi). Car rental recommended.

Left above, the inn and grounds are checked out by Martha the dog. Below, the common room.

The pool has an ocean view.

Breakfast features West Indian-style oatmeal.

A guest room.

FIREFLY HOUSE

A harvest of collectibles

If you want small, you can't get much tinier than Mustique, a privately owned island that plays seasonal host to the rich and famous. On the entire island there's one hotel, a collection of exclusive villa rentals, and—thank goodness—one affordable B&B.

Firefly House was built two decades ago as one of the first estate homes on Mustique. The two-story guest house is perched on the edge of a steep hillside overlooking Britannia Bay. At the entry level is an open-air living room of vaulted hardwood ceilings and rustic stone walls, decorated with overstuffed cushions, Balinese artwork, and other collectibles from owner Billy Mitchell's twenty years of sailing around the world. From the breakfast table and balcony you can view the bay and neighboring celebrity homes. Billy will proudly point out that her view is better than David Bowie's and that it was "Mick" who first suggested she open her home to guests as he needed more room for his visiting friends.

A spiral staircase leads down to four guest rooms, which also have thick stone walls and floorboards that peek right through to the hillside. But various touches of refinement—soft white fabrics, whimsical, hand-painted lampshades, and gauzy mosquito

Left above, the living room, with its unique stone construction. Below, the view from a balcony.

netting over the beds—balance out the rusticity, creating a surprisingly charming air. Two of the rooms have a whole wall and bathroom open to the harbor view, allowing the foliage to creep in.

Things are very informal here: There are no room keys, no special time for breakfast, no formal introduction. You can walk everywhere, and Basil's Bar—the only affordable restaurant on the island—is just a short hike down the steep hill. When returning at night, you'll see why this guest house was named Firefly by the little twinkling lights that guide you home.

FIREFLY HOUSE, Box 349, Mustique, St. Vincent, The Grenadines; (809) 456-3414; (809) 456-3514; Billy & Gala Mitchell, owners. Open all year. Four rooms, all with private baths. Air conditioning in two rooms. High season rates: $90 to $107; low season: $60 to $80, including full breakfast. Children welcome; smoking allowed; French spoken; Visa/MasterCard. Macaroni Beach nearby. Basil's Bar and Cotton House recommended for dining.

DIRECTIONS: Mustique can be reached by air from St. Vincent. Firefly House is two minutes from the airport and will arrange transportation. Car rental not necessary.

Details in a guest room.

The main building.

Pamela Barry, the owner.

GOLDEN ROCK ESTATE

An old sugar plantation

The islands of Nevis (prounounced "NEE-vis") and neighboring St. Kitts are well known for their historic plantation inns. Golden Rock Estate, which has preserved many of its old stone ruins on the slopes of rain-forested Nevis Peak, is run by Pamela Barry, a direct descendant of the original owners.

Pam's ancestors first established this sugar plantation in 1805. After the sugar industry declined, her grandfather moved the family to the U.S. where Pamela was born. She returned to Nevis in the 60s and gradually took over as co-owner and manager of her ancestral home.

The main "long house" has a country castle feel with its cool, thick stone walls. While the old wing houses a cozy bar (where Ralston, the bartender, fixes one of the best rum punches in the Caribbean) and inviting library, the new wing contains a game room and restaurant that serves hearty West Indian dinners. Just outside is a peaceful courtyard brightened by multi-colored bougainvillea. From here you can gaze up at the every-changing clouds on the mountain while having breakfast, lunch or afternoon tea.

Dominating the hill is an old stone mill which has been converted into a romantic suite. Other guest accommodations are in functional concrete bungalows scattered over the hillside. Each bungalow is divided into two bamboo-furnished units with semi-private balconies.

One of the highlights at Golden Rock are the African green monkeys that thrive on the grounds. They can best be spotted from a trail that begins at the inn and leads into a jungle of jumbie bead

Left, the tower containing the Windmill Suite overlooks the breakfast courtyard.

vines, tree ferns, and breadfruit trees. It's exciting to watch them swing blithely from branch to branch, munching on mangos and throwing them carelessly to the ground.

GOLDEN ROCK ESTATE, Box 493, Gingerland, Nevis, West Indies; (809) 469-3346; Fax (809) 469-2113; Pamela Barry, owner. Represented by ITR at (800) 223-9815. Open all year. Fourteen rooms and one suite, all with private baths. No air conditioning. High season rates: $179 to $203; low season: $94 to $118, including full breakfast. MAP plan available. Children welcome; smoking allowed; Visa/MasterCard/American Express. Nature trail, rain forest hike, restaurant, tennis, and swimming pool all on premises. Free shuttle to four nearby beaches.

DIRECTIONS: on the southeast side of Nevis, 30 minutes from the airport (about $20 by taxi). Car rental recommended for exploring the island.

The bar area.

Celia and James Gaskell, owners.

MONTPELIER PLANTATION INN

Princess Di slept here

This very secluded country retreat is run by gracious hosts Celia and James Gaskell. Originally from England, the Gaskells built Montpelier Plantation Inn on the site of an old Nevis sugar plantation. Though only thirty years old, the inn looks authentically historic, with an air of British refinement that has compelled even Princess Diana to vacation here.

At the entrance is a gnarled, ancient fig tree and stone steps leading up to the Great Hall—a baronial-style gathering room with thick stone walls and high, arched ceilings. Off of this room is a cozy library/card room. Elsewhere on the grounds are

Left above, the Great Hall and below, the interior, with its bar and lounge.

guest cottages, a swimming pool, tennis courts, and various relics of the plantation days, including a large stone mill.

The one-story guest cottages—each divided into two units—are light, airy, and understatedly elegant, with delicate four-poster beds and tasteful English floral fabrics of pale green, coral, and white. Every room has a private patio and luxurious bathroom.

Dinner at Monpelier is a civilized affair: guests dress for dinner and gather in the bar of the Great Hall for cocktails while the Gaskells pass around hors d'oeuvres. Then everyone is led outside to the dining terrace where intimate tables are prettily set with candles. The excellent four-course dinners might start with pâté and a crab tart in lobster sauce, followed by rack of lamb in mint sauce, and finally some melt-in-your-mouth mango cheesecake. At the end of this repast, everyone retires to the chintz-covered couches of the Great Hall where coffee and sweets are already set at various tables.

The copious, English-style breakfasts, served on another open-air terrace, include Johnny cakes with lemon curd, a choice of eggs, pancakes, or French toast, broiled tomatoes and bacon—or even kippers, if you want them.

MONTPELIER PLANTATION INN, P.O. Box 474, Nevis, West Indies; (809) 469-3462; Fax (809) 469-2932; James & Celia Gaskell, owners. Represented by E&M Associates at (212) 599-8280. Closed August 15 to October 2. Sixteen rooms and one suite, all with private baths. No air conditioning. High season rates: $220 to $280; low season: $150 to $180, including full breakfast. Children welcome; smoking allowed; French spoken; Visa/MasterCard. Tennis court and swimming pool on premises. Pinney's Beach (free shuttle available), deep sea fishing, snorkeling and windsurfing nearby. Montpelier Plantation Inn and Hermitage recommended for dining.

DIRECTIONS: ten miles from airport (about $18 by taxi). Car rental recommended for exploring the island.

A typical guest room.

A guest cottage.

The typically Spanish interior courtyard.

The marble floored elegance of Suite 104.

HOTEL CASA SAN JOSÉ

Grandly restored

Since the 1993 quincentennial celebrations marking its discovery by Columbus, Old San Juan has undergone an amazing transformation. Over half of the crumbling old buildings have been restored and are now occupied by upscale art galleries, bistros, and boutiques. The former seediness of the narrow streets has vanished, but its colorful character is still much alive.

Hotel Casa San José perhaps best exemplifies the sophisticated rebirth of Old San Juan. This dignified nineteenth-century townhouse sits unobtrusively in the heart of town, identified only by a simple brass plaque. Inside, the graceful reception hall glows with light marble floors and a stunning chandelier. The three-story tiled staircase winds around a skylit courtyard of creamy stone archways and bubbling fountain. Throughout the hotel are soothing tones of pale green and cream, contrasted by rust-toned, Turkish kilim rugs spread over the cool marble floors.

Every room is a visual delight, thanks to the decorating skills of Simone Mehta, wife of owner and leading San Juan hotelier Jag Mehta. The

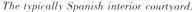

Left, the Grand Salon.

antique furnishings and four-poster beds are covered with luxurious, pale fabrics while the walls are hung with rich tapestries and fine, sepia-toned prints. Though each guest room is highly unique, Suite 104 is distinguished by its balustraded balconies that open, Romeo-and-Juliet-style, onto the interior courtyard.

On the second level is a thousand-square-foot grand salon that is reminiscent of a ballroom, complete with grand piano, marble floors, and gilt mirrors. Here you can read on one of the plump couches and enjoy your complimentary evening cocktail. The adjoining breakfast room is accented by chairs covered in red and white country French fabric. The continental breakfast is beautifully presented by a gracious staff.

HOTEL CASA SAN JOSÉ, 159 San José Street, Old San Juan, Puerto Rico 00901; (809) 723-1212; (809) 723-7620; Jag Mehta, owner; Ms. Maruja Hernaiz, manager. Represented by Robert Reid Associates at (800) 223-6510. Open all year. Ten rooms and suites, all with private baths and air conditioning. High season rates: $215 to $235 low season: $170 to $190, including continental breakfast and afternoon tea. Children under 12 not allowed; smoking permitted; Spanish spoken. All credit cards accepted. Historic walking tours, museums, art galleries, shopping, and cruise docks nearby. Amadeus and La Mallorquina recommended for dining.

DIRECTIONS: in the heart of Old San Juan, 20 minutes from the airport (about $15 by taxi). Validated parking one block away. Car rental not necessary.

The front of the inn seen from the street.

EL CANARIO INN

In a bustling neighborhood

This modest, Spanish-style hotel was built in the 1930s as a private villa just one block from San Juan's famous Condado Beach. When the owners passed the home on to their daughter as a wedding gift in the 1960s, she and her husband converted it into a bed and breakfast inn. Twenty years later it was bought by Keith Olson, an American who now owns two more B&B hotels in the Condado area—El Canario by the Lagoon, and El Canario by the Sea.

Of the three hotels, El Canario Inn is the most atmospheric. Its narrow, three-story, melon-pink facade is decorated with terra cotta-tiled roofs and ornate wrought iron grills. The small lobby and lounge are pleasant and inviting, with black and white checkered floors, white wicker furnishings, and tropical plants. A narrow brick courtyard leads to a small hot tub in the back.

The bedrooms are clean, functional, and motel-like, with tile floors, pastel floral spreads, and simple rattan furnishings. They offer all the basic

Left, the reception lounge.

amenities—phones, television, room safes, and air conditioning—plus a continental breakfast and morning newspaper.

Though unassuming, El Canario's moderate rates, convenient location, and congenial atmosphere make it one of the best values in San Juan.

EL CANARIO INN, 1317 Ashford Avenue, Condado, Puerto Rico 00907; (800) 742-4276; (809) 722-3861; Fax (809) 722-0391; Keith Olson; owner; José Colón Hernández, manager. Open all year. Twenty-five rooms, all with private baths and air conditioning. High season rates: $75 to $95; low season: $55 to $70, including continental breakfast. Children welcome; smoking allowed; Spanish spoken; all credit cards accepted. Condado Beach, casinos, convention center, and many restaurants nearby.

DIRECTIONS: in the heart of the Condado resort area of San Juan, 15 minutes from the airport.

A guest room.

The pool and reception building.

The beach and ocean from the reception building balcony.

HORNED DORSET PRIMAVERA

Blissful idleness

Although not a typical bed and breakfast, the Horned Dorset Primavera is the one of most luxurious and romantic hideaways on Puerto Rico. Secluded on a lush stretch of the island's west coast, this intimate hotel was lovingly created by Harold Davies and Kingsley Wratten—both former literature professors and founders of an upstate New York restaurant called the Horned Dorset. Every detail here—from the library selections, to the tasteful décor, to the gracious staff—has the mark of intelligence and vision.

As you enter the unobtrusive gates, you will feel enveloped in a cloak of cool greenery. Gorgeous gardens surround the hotel with intensely-colored tropical flowers dripping from the trees. The white, Mediterranean-style reception building and its guest annexes are highlighted by graceful arches, pillars, and classically-balustraded balconies overlooking a wide expanse of placid ocean.

Off the reception area is an inviting, wicker-filled library and bar where Pompidou, the resident macaw, peers curiously from his cage during the evening cocktail hour. Outside is an open-air breakfast terrace, and above that is a marvelous dining room which radiates with romance at night, its hurricane lamps softly glowing, tables elegantly set with polished silver, and a classical guitarist performing in the background.

Guest quarters are grouped in six villas over the water and on the hillside. While the oceanfront bedrooms are especially wonderful, most rooms feature four-poster beds, a sitting area, private balconies, and ultra-luxurious marble bathrooms.

Aside from a narrow bib of beach, the wide, elegant swimming pool is the only "activity" found

Left above, the hillside guest quarters. Below, the library and bar.

on the grounds. Idleness is the general design here, and most of the guests are willing and blissful participants.

HORNED DORSET PRIMAVERA, P.O. Box 1132, Rincón, Puerto Rico 00677; (809) 823-4030; (809) 823-4050; Fax (809) 823-5580; Harold L. Davis & Kingsley D. Wratten, owners. Relais and Chateaux member. Open all year. Twenty-two rooms, all with private baths and air conditioning. High season rates: $325; low season: $190, with continental breakfast available for $10 extra. No children under 12; smoking not permitted in dining room; Spanish and French spoken; all credit cards accepted. No activities at hotel. Golf, tennis, fishing, scuba diving, and surfing nearby. Restaurant on premises.

DIRECTIONS: on the west coast of Puerto Rico, south of Rincón, 20 minutes from Mayaguez or Aguadilla Airports (about $20 by taxi). Approximately 1 hour from San Juan Airport. Car rental recommended for exploring the island.

Room 2 oceanfront suite.

CAPTAIN'S QUARTERS

High in the mountains above the sea

Of the few lodgings found on tiny Saba (pronounced "SAY-bah"), Captain's Quarters is the main place to stay. Situated in Windwardside, an adorable mountain village of steep, narrow lanes, this nineteenth-century sea captain's home and its cluster of guest quarters are built with typical Saban charm, the whitewashed walls trimmed with dark green gingerbread and red roofs.

The swimming pool, bar, and reception area are perched on a volcanic cliff fifteen hundred feet above the sea. Terraced above that is an open-air dining pavilion (which will soon be moved to the bar area), cozy television lounge, and several guest houses with individual balconies on each. The prettiest guest quarters are found in the original Victorian house behind the restaurant. Room Two, for instance, is a cheery delight, with lofty white cathedral ceilings, Oriental carpets over wood floors, and a flouncy pink canopied bed. The high elevation of Windwardside, its refreshing sea breezes, and an abundance of shuttered windows keep all the guest rooms naturally cool.

This is the only establishment on the island where breakfast is included, in addition to a complimentary welcome drink in the bar. Be sure to try one of the house specialties—a Divers Down-Bottoms Up or Saba Mama—both made with the locally-made Saban spice liqueur.

There are no locks on the doors here. With only a thousand residents on the entire island, everyone knows everyone. The locals, mostly of Scottish descent, are extraordinarily sweet and friendly. Just stroll around the town for a day or so, and you'll meet nearly all of them.

CAPTAIN'S QUARTERS, Windwardside, Saba, Netherlands Antilles; (011) 599-462201; Fax (011) 599-462377; Calvin Holm & Richard Holm, owners. Represented by Captain's Quarters Sales Office at (212) 289-6031. Open all year. Ten rooms, all with private baths; 2 rooms with air conditioning. High season rates: $95 to $150; low season: $95 to $125, including full breakfast. Children welcome; smoking allowed; Visa/MasterCard. Dive packages available. Hiking and fantastic diving on the island. Captain's Quarters, Lollipops, and Brigadoon recommended for dining.

DIRECTIONS: in the village of Windwardside, 15 minutes from the airport (about $5 by taxi). Car rental not necessary.

Left above, the guest quarters, with the original house on the left. Below, the swimming pool and its view of the water.

The dining terrace.

Room 2 has a canopied bed.

JULIANA'S

A wide choice of accommodations

This fresh, tidy collection of guest rooms and apartments is located right next to the Captain's Quarters. Although not technically a bed and breakfast (breakfast is available at their café for an extra charge), Juliana's is an enchanting place to stay.

There is quite a variety of accommodations here—bedrooms, apartments, and a historic cottage—housed in several white buildings with red roofs that are trimmed with dark green and an abundance of Saban gingerbread filigree. Most of the guest rooms have private balconies overlooking either the well-tended garden or the sea, far below. The bedrooms are decorated in tiled floors, pastel fabrics, and simple furnishings—nothing fancy, but pin-neat.

Saban-born owner Juliana Johnson is a sweet, charming hostess. She and her husband Franklin run the guest quarters while their son, Griffin, operates the Tropics Cafe, which is set off to one side on a terrace above the pool.

Nicknamed "The Unspoiled Queen," Saba is an

Adjoining cottages.

extraordinary little island composed of sheer volcanic peaks and charming gingerbread cottages perched precariously on the cliffs. The only horizontal surface on the entire island is a band-aid strip of an airport—one of the shortest in the world—which is accessed by a precipitous switchback road.

JULIANA'S, Windwardside, Saba, Netherlands Antilles; (011) 599-462269; Fax (011) 599-462389; Juliana & Franklin Johnson, owners. Represented by ITR at (800) 223-9815. Open all year. Nine rooms, one suite, and one cottage, all with private baths. No air conditioning. High season rates: $75 to $125; low season: $60 to $100, with breakfast available for an extra charge. Children under 12 free; smoking allowed; Visa/MasterCard. Pool on premises. Diving and hiking nearby.

DIRECTIONS: in the village of Windwardside, 15 minutes from the airport (about $5 by taxi). Car rental not necessary.

Flossie's Cottage.

The swimming pool.

Living room of Villa Two.

LES CASTELETS

A commanding view of St. Barts

This auberge-style gem of an inn is poised high on a quiet mountain top, commanding a spectacular view of the entire western length of St. Barts with its undulating fingers of soft green hills stretching out to the lapis and emerald sea.

The restaurant, guest rooms, and villas of Les Castelets appear as if they were transplanted straight from Provençal. In fact, everything—the décor, fabrics, architecture, food, service—is thoroughly yet unpretentiously French. While even the smaller guest rooms over the restaurant are quite lovely, the private villas are truly marvelous. Staggered at different levels on the hillside, with a triangular plunge pool in between, each two-story villa has an inspiring ambience and panoramic view that can't be beat.

Villa Two, for example, is distinguished by a two-story living room with marble floors, wood-beamed cathedral ceilings, and furnishings covered in rich designer fabrics. Upstairs is a bedroom

Villa Two.

and bathroom with attic-like ceilings. High arched windows and French doors open from the living room onto a long, wicker-filled balcony, which takes full advantage of the marvelous vista.

Les Castelets has been owned and run for more than twenty years by Geneviève Jouany, a serene Frenchwoman who exemplifies the refined taste that prevails throughout. This year she is turning over management to someone new and sending her chef to the best cooking school in the world. Her restaurant is considered one of the finest on St. Barts. Among the nightly specialties are duck carpaccio, locally-caught lobster, roasted scallops with julienne of endive, chocolate marquise, and flambéed mangoes.

Though it has no beach, Les Castelets is one of the most memorable hostelries in the entire Caribbean. And the view—*c'est magnifique*!

LES CASTELETS, B.P. 60, 97133 St. Barthélemy, French West Indies; (011) 590-276173; (011) 590-277880; Fax (011) 590-278527; Geneviève Jouany, owner; Jean-Claude & Iréne Laugeois, managers. Represented by Ralph Locke Island, Inc. at (800) 223-1108. Closed September 1 to November 1. Six rooms, including two two-bedroom villas, all with private baths and air conditioning. High season rates: $75 to $315; low season: $70 to $300, including continental breakfast. Small children not encouraged; smoking allowed; French and Spanish spoken; Visa/MasterCard/American Express. Governours Beach and Shell Beach nearby. Les Castelets, Maya, La Banane, and Marigot Bay Club recommended for dining.

DIRECTIONS: just outside Gustavia, 1.5 steep, winding miles from the airport (about $12 by taxi). Try to rent a car or Minimoke from the airport upon arrival.

A two-story living room.

Right, the breathtaking view from the pool.

The bedroom of Villa Two.

St. Jean Beach, right at the door of the inn.

HOTEL FILAO BEACH

Color coordinated

Hotel Filao Beach could be recommended for its outstanding beach alone. A perfect crescent of dazzling white sand and azure sea, St. Jean Beach is ideal for sunning and swimming.

But it's all the extra touches that really count here. It begins from the moment you arrive, when the receptionist personally escorts you through the landscaped, flowery pathways to your cottage room. On the coffee table is a welcome note with a tiny fresh flower affixed to the envelope, set before a complimentary bottle of Moet & Chandon *petite liquorelle*—a sublime hazelnut-flavored liqueur.

The bedroom and sitting areas are decorated in floral pastels and pale rattan, accented by fresh-cut anthuriums. They are all equipped with cable television, telephone, quiet air conditioning, mini-refrigerator, candles, bottled water, and ice. Each private balcony has a table that hides plates and cups in its cupboard—ideal for private little picnics. In the bathrooms are a host of toiletries, plus a hair dryer, piles of fluffy towels, a close-up mirror, and deluxe shower. Also provided are evening turn-down service with terry slippers placed by your bed. The next morning, breakfast—which includes a separate pot of coffee for each guest—appears discreetly on your balcony.

Guest rooms—each named after a different French château—are grouped randomly in single-story cottages around a casual, open-air café/bar, and tiled swimming pool which overlooks the beach. Bathing suits and shorts are *de rigueur* here. Even with all the luxuries, the atomosphere is friendly and informal.

Manager Pierre Verdier has been running hotels in the Caribbean for more than twenty years, so he knows how much difference all these little touches

Left, a guest cottage just a few steps from the beach.

A color coordinated guest room.

make. It comes as no surprise that Filao Beach is a member of Relais & Châteaux, a worldwide association of privately owned, unique hotels that are known for their profusion of amenities.

HOTEL FILAO BEACH, St. Jean Bay, Box 667 Cedex, 91099 St. Barthélemy, French West Indies; (011) 590-276484; Fax (011) 590-276224; Pierre Verdier, manager. Closed from September to mid-October. Thirty rooms, all with private baths and air conditioning. High season rates: $318 to $582, including full breakfast; low season: $180 to $345, including continental breakfast. Children welcome; smoking allowed; French and Spanish spoken; all credit cards accepted. St. Jean Beach, swimming pool and snorkeling on premises. Sailing, windsurfing, tennis, scuba diving, and horseback riding nearby. New Born, François Plantation, and Maya recommended for dining.

DIRECTIONS: on St. Jean Beach, 1.5 miles from the airport. Free hotel shuttle offered by prior arrangement.

A symphony of water colors.

The view from the modern swimming pool.

FRANÇOIS PLANTATION

A tropical paradise of beautiful gardens

This colorful cluster of charming cottages—painted purple, turquoise, and mustard yellow—cling to the side of a steep hillside above Flamande Bay. Except for the sound of wind chimes, morning doves, and gurgling fountains, all is quiet and peaceful here.

An intimate, family-run inn, François Plantation draws a loyal clientele year after year. Owner François Beret, who has lived in the Caribbean for over twenty years, built the inn from scratch with his wife Françoise. He tends the beautiful gardens himself, and even during times of drought manages to maintain the lush foliage. From the open-air restaurant, bar and reception area, guests can overlook a tropical paradise of bright blossoms—bougainvillea and hibiscus of every color—inter-

Left above, colorful guest cottages. Below, the view from one of the cottages.

spersed with uniquely-sculpted fountains and interesting paths of tilework.

Each bungalow cottage is simply furnished in mahogany, with West Indian artwork on the walls and amenities such as televisions, telephones, room safes, and mini-bars. Eight of the cottages have inviting private terraces with an ocean view while four other cottage terraces face the garden. At the top of the hill, above the rooftops, is a swimming pool with panoramic ocean view.

The veranda-style, rattan-filled dining room at François Plantation is pricey but well regarded on St. Barts. France melds sublimely with the Caribbean in the unusual delicacies offered here, such as iced shellfish soup scented with citrus fruits and ginger, or tournedos of ostrich served with a purée of island vegetables and Jamaican peppers.

FRANÇOIS PLANTATION, Colombier, 97133 St. Barthélemy, French West Indies; (011) 590-277882; Fax (011) 590-276126; François & Françoise Beret, owners. Closed from August 15 to October 15. Twelve bungalows, all with private baths and air conditioning. High season rates: $250 to $400; low season: $180 to $240, including full breakfast. Children can be accommodated in two bungalows; smoking allowed; French and Spanish spoken; Visa/MasterCard/American Express. Flamande Beach nearby. François Plantation Restaurant recommended for dining.

DIRECTIONS: in Colombier, on northwest St. Barts, 5 minutes from the airport (about $15 by taxi). Car rental recommended upon arrival.

Breakfast tray of banana pancakes.

Detail in the Rose Room.

SPRAT HALL PLANTATION

A museum of family heirlooms

The drowsy, moss-covered landscape of western St. Croix (pronounced "Croy") is reminiscent of the Old South, and the French colonial great house of Sprat Hall Plantation fits perfectly into its antebellum-like setting. Dating to 1650, it is indeed the oldest intact plantation house in the Virgin Islands. Judy Young, a fifteenth generation Croixian, grew up at Sprat Hall while her parents ran it as an inn. Now Judy, her husband, and son have taken over innkeeping duties.

The interior of the great house is like a living museum, filled to the brim with family heirlooms. Though it could use a bit of a facelift, there is an air of faded romance throughout the house, enhanced by an abundance of lace, candles, and artfully arranged fresh flowers. Nowhere is this more evident than in the Wedgewood blue and white dining room, where the tables are covered with white embroidered linens, antique hurricane lamps, blue-and-white ancestral china, and gold cutlery.

SPRAT HALL PLANTATION, Box 645, Frederiksted, U.S. Virgin Islands 00841; (800) 843-3584; (809) 772-0305; Mark & Judy Young, owners. Open all year. Fourteen rooms, six with kitchenettes, all with private baths; air conditioning in all rooms but the great house. High season rates: $110 to $210; low season: $100 to $170, including full breakfast in rooms without kitchenettes. Children welcome in efficiencies or one-bedroom house; smoking allowed in specified rooms only; Spanish spoken; American Express accepted. Horseback riding on premises. Beaches, snorkeling, hiking, bird watching, museums, and botanical gardens nearby. Dinner available by prior arrangement. Blue Moon, Sprat Hall Beach Club, and Cafe du Soleil also recommended for dining.

DIRECTIONS: just north of Frederiksted, 15 minutes from the airport (about $5 per person by taxi). Car rental recommended.

Left above, the plantation Great House. Below, the Rose Room, full of antiques.

In addition to her love for antiques, lace, and flowers, Judy has a passion for horses. She keeps nearly a dozen fine horses in stables on the grounds, which is a big draw for equestrians.

The most romantic guest rooms are on the second floor of the great house. The Rose Room is particularly spacious, with dark green floors and shutters, pink walls, and a sitting area with old mahogany planters chairs. Guests staying here or in the sea view rooms adjacent to the great house will have breakfast delivered to the door on an exquisitely set tray. A typical breakfast might include banana pancakes with homemade guava syrup and flower garnishes fresh from the garden.

The dining room.

The hotel from the street.

The pool and breakfast area.

PINK FANCY

Guest rooms are modern, fresh, and brightly furnished

Though not in a particularly "fancy" area of Christensted, Pink Fancy is a clean, cheerful place to stay. Its pink shutters, small-paned windows, and candy-striped awnings make it visually inviting, and the atmosphere is quite comfortable, especially for families.

The accommodations consist of four historic buildings—the oldest a 1780 Danish townhouse—that are built on several levels around a patio with a swimming pool. Continental breakfast is served daily at an honor bar by the pool, and guests spend a lot of time out here lounging around, which creates a congenial, house-party type of atmosphere.

Though the stone foundations make the façade look old-fashioned, the interiors of the guest rooms are modern, fresh, and brightly furnished with rattan, West Indian fabrics, cable televisions, and kitchenettes. Each room has the whimsical name of a different St. Croix estate, such as "Upper Love," "Hard Labor," "Bonne Esperence," and "Humbug."

Christensted, settled by the Danes in 1733, is a picturesque harbor town. Its colorful Danish buildings were badly damaged during Hurricane Hugo but they have since been mostly restored. Pink Fancy is situated just two blocks from the water and within an easy walk of downtown. Be sure to visit the harborfront—especially Fort Christiansvaern and the Customs House—which has been designated a historic area. Tiny Buck Island Reef, a short ferry ride from town, offers an excellent beach and snorkeling.

PINK FANCY, 27 Prince St., Christensted, St. Croix, U.S. Virgin Islands; (809) 778-8460; Fax (809) 773-6448; Dixie Ann Tang Yuk, manager. Open all year. Twelve rooms, all with private baths and air conditioning. High season rates: $90 to $120; low season: $75 to $90, including continental breakfast. Children welcome; smoking allowed; all credit cards accepted. Tennis, golf, snorkeling at Buck Island National Monument, and duty-free shopping in historic Christensted nearby. Kim's Restaurant, Kendrick's, and Harvey's Restaurant recommended for dining.

DIRECTIONS: in Christensted, 25 minutes from the airport (about $5 per person by taxi). Car rental recommended for exploring St. Croix.

The living-dining room.

HILTY HOUSE INN

Originally designed for large-scale entertaining

Set on a bluff just outside Christiansted, this lovely villa was built in the 1960s over the ruins of an eighteenth-century rum factory. An entrepreneur and developer designed the house for large-scale entertaining, with an enormous great room, huge kitchen, guest cottages, and graceful swimming pool. After Hurricane Hugo hit St. Croix several years ago, the present owners, Hugh and Jacquie Hoare-Ward, left their corporate jobs to move here permanently and turn Hilty House into a bed and breakfast inn.

Hugh, an Englishman, and Jacquie, who is Lebanese, are genuinely warm, engaging hosts.

Around happy hour, guests often gravitate to the pool terrace for conversation while Hugh cheerfully fixes drinks. Jacquie makes her own breads, jams and marmalades for breakfast, and entertains up to thirty people once a week with her Mediterranean dinners.

Of the four bedrooms in the main house, the Blue Room and Pink Room are most appealing. Both feature hand-painted Italian tile floors, wicker furnishing, pretty designer linens, and arched windows, set against a background of fresh white walls.

Jacquie and Hugh Hoare-Ward with Echo the dog.

Venetian chandeliers provide a delightful contrast to the glass block showers in the bathroom. The three guest cottages near the main house are equally pleasing to the eye. One cottage—the former cookhouse—has a restored kitchen with its original hearth still intact, plus a unique porch that is screened in with staggered slats, keeping it private yet breezy.

The focal point of the main house is the thousand-square-foot Great Room, its white, skylit décor punctuated by dramatic accents of black and brown. Other common areas include a cozy library with television and VCR, the pool area, and gallery—a long patio where breakfast is served.

HILTY HOUSE INN, P.O. Box 26077, Gallows Bay, St. Croix, U.S. Virgin Islands 00824; (809) 773-2594; Fax (809) 773-2594; Jacquie & Hugh Hoare-Ward, owners. Open all year. Four rooms and three self-catering cottages, all with private baths. No air conditioning. High season rates: $75 to $99; low season: $60 to $85, including continental breakfast for guests in the main house (and breakfast provisions for one day in the cottages). Children over 12 welcome; smoking not allowed in house; French and Arabic spoken; No credit cards. Rain forest, scuba diving, snorkeling, and museums nearby. Tutto Bene, Indies, and Kim's recommended for dining.

DIRECTIONS: near Christiansted, 25 minutes from the airport (about $5 per person by taxi). Car rental recommended.

A tropical fruit tray of mango, papaya, and kiwi.

Right, the cool elegance of the Blue Room.

The Mooshay Bay Publick House.

THE OLD GIN HOUSE

Antique-filled rooms

About fifteen minutes by air from St. Maarten is tiny St. Eustatius (commonly referred to as Statia), which is fondly remembered in American history as the only Caribbean island to provide much needed supplies for the Revolutionaries. The British retaliated by sending Admiral George Rodney to capture and ransack the entire island of its riches.

Whenever travelers tell this story of Statia, talk invariably turns to The Old Gin House. This inn

Guest rooms are filled with antiques.

actually consists of two atmospheric buildings which are across the street from each other. The main building—called the Mooshay Bay Publick House—is an authentic reconstruction of an eighteenth-century building which once housed a cotton gin. Built of old bricks which were once used for ballast on sailing ships, Mooshay Bay serves as the evening bar while upstairs is a library with games and videos. Fourteen of its antique-filled guest rooms overlook the swimming pool while six others are across the street in The Old Gin House—an oceanfront building which also houses a bar and patio dining area.

Outside the door is a black sand beach where guests can swim, snorkel or dive among the old sunken seawalls and warehouses. The old-fashioned town of Oranjebaai is full of narrow streets, stone walls, and historic buildings.

THE OLD GIN HOUSE, Oranjebaai, Lowertown, St. Eustatius, Netherlands Antilles; (011) 599-382319; (011) 599-382555; John May, owner. Represented by E&M Associates at (800) 223-9832. Open all year. Twenty rooms, all with private baths. No air conditioning. High season rates: $85 to $115; low season: $50 to $75, with breakfast available for an extra charge. No children under 10; smoking allowed; Dutch, German, and French spoken; all credit cards accepted. Resturant on premises. La Maison Sur La Plage and King's Well also recommended for dining.

DIRECTIONS: on the sea, 1.2 miles from the airport (about $3.50 per person by taxi).

The bar aims to please.

CRUZ INN

St. John's only bed & breakfast

The Cruz Inn is functional and far from luxurious, but it's one of the most affordable places to stay—and the only bed and breakfast—on St. John. Set a few blocks from the ferry dock, this West Indian-style guest house is within easy walking distance of downtown Cruz Bay.

The inn is composed of three buildings built of white and pistachio green stucco. Though they vary in what few amenities they offer—some have air conditioning (which you should request as it can get very hot in Cruz Bay) and a few have private baths—all of the guest rooms are quite basic, with very little in the way of décor. The Papaya Suite, with its two bedrooms, private bath, full kitchen, air conditioning, and view, is the most requested.

On the second floor of the main building is a pleasant, open-air, bamboo-trimmed bar which looks upon Enighed Pond and the ocean beyond. Movies are shown here twice weekly, and this is where the daily continental breakfast is served.

The atmosphere is congenial, in part because of longtime manager Gayle Gosselin, who is a real people person. She has lived on St. John for nearly fifteen years and still loves every part of it. For next-to-heaven snorkeling, Gayle sends her guests to Cinnamon Bay or Trunk Bay, both accessed by a winding, fifteen-minute drive of spectacular overlooks. "The first time I drive right by those overlooks, that's when I'll leave," says Gayle. "I take forever to go anywhere."

Every Fourth of July week, Carnival takes place in Cruz Bay, an event which draws lots of sailboats and day-trippers from St. Thomas who wander among the streetside food stands sampling such West Indian foods as mutton, kalaloo, coconut tarts, tamarind juice, and maubi, a local juice.

CRUZ INN, 277 Enighed, Box 797, Cruz Bay, St. John, U.S. Virgin Islands 00831; (800) 666-7688; (809) 693-8688; Fax (809) 693-8590; Lonnie Willis, owner; Gayle Gosselin, manager. Open all year. Nine rooms and five apartments, some with shared baths. Air conditioning optional in six rooms for $10 extra. High season rates: $55 to $95; low season: $50 to $85, including continental breakfast. Children welcome; smoking allowed; all credit cards accepted. Sugar mill ruins, Ram's Head National Park, and fantastic snorkeling nearby. Lime Inn, Fish Trap, Etta's, and Chateau Bordeaux recommended for dining.

DIRECTIONS: in Cruz Bay, several blocks from the ferry dock (about $2 per person by taxi). Car rental not necessary.

Street view of the inn.

View from the bar area.

OTTLEY'S PLANTATION

Where everything is done right

Nestled at the foot of verdant Mt. Liamuiga on St. Kitts, this lovingly restored sugar estate—built in 1707 by Drewry Ottley of England—has a luxuriant sense of space rarely found in the modern world. Sweeping gracefully down toward the sea are thirty-five acres of expansive, manicured lawns and tropical foliage—massive trees, exotic orchids, and velvety red hibiscus.

The proud centerpiece is a colonial-style great house, painted in crisp yellow with two stories of delicately-trimmed wraparound verandas. The great house contains fifteen extra-spacious, rattan-furnished guest rooms, a library, and inviting reception area. The second-story bedrooms feature airy cathedral ceilings. Heavy, louvered, plantation-style shutters allow the ocean breezes to waft refreshingly through the rooms. Other guest quarters are housed in several gray stone cottages adjacent to the great house. The English Cottage, with its pretty mullioned windows, was once the old cotton house.

The splendidly groomed grounds were made for strolling, especially in the early mornings when exotic bird calls fill the air and mysterious clouds blanket the mountain. A short walk down the hill brings you to a sixty-five-foot spring-fed swimming pool which has been cleverly built into the ruins of the boiling house. Adjoining this is the Palm Court Restaurant, which serves gourmet New Island-style cuisine and popular Sunday brunches.

Ottley's Plantation Inn was created six years ago by two couples—The Keusches and Lowells—who previously ran a family book store chain in the Northeast. With Ottley's, they have managed to preserve the slow pace of the colonial days without sacrificing any modern comforts. They provide their

Left, the Great House from the front gardens.

Room 5.

guests with the sort of personal attention and surprising little niceties that make one feel pampered and cared for. This is one of those rare places where everything is done right.

OTTLEY'S PLANTATION INN, Box 345, Basseterre, St. Kitts, West Indies; (800) 772-3039; (809) 465-7234; Fax (809) 465-4760; Art & Ruth Keusch, Marty & Nancy Lowell, owners. Open all year. Nine rooms and three cottages, all with private baths and air conditioning. High season rates: $250 to $335; low season: $190 to $235, including breakfast. MAP plan and honeymoon packages available. Inquire about children; smoking allowed; Visa/MasterCard/Amerian Express. Brimstone Hill Fortress, batik factory, rainforests, beaches, golf, casino, and water sports nearby. Royal Palm Restaurant recommended for dining.

DIRECTIONS: on northeast St. Kitts, 15 minutes from the airport (about $15 by taxi). Complimentary airport transfer for stays of 4 days or longer.

The English Cottage.

The pool and dining area.

The old sugar mill is now a charming guest suite.

RAWLINS PLANTATION

Sophistication of a country house

Rawlins Plantation was originally among the three hundred sugar estates that operated on St. Kitts. From 1690 up until 1970 the property produced sugar and a little sea island cotton. Though Rawlins was restored and run as a small inn for ten years, it wasn't until 1989, when Hurricane Hugo hit, that the former plantation was refurbished and upgraded to its present state of elegance.

Set on twelve acres of rolling hills is the great house, its bar affording a panoramic view of the cane fields and sea. Most of the guest rooms are in cottages that are tastefully appointed in colorful English fabrics, antiques, and four-poster beds. The original sugar mill, which once ground sugar cane, has been converted into a charming suite. Various pieces of old sugar-making machinery are scattered about the grounds.

The inn is run by gracious hosts Paul Rawson, a much-traveled English hotelier, and his Kittian-

Left above, the original plantation Great House. Below, the pool, set on the estate's grounds, attracts friendly egrets.

born wife, Claire. Claire's family, The Mallalieus, are one of the oldest, most prominent families on the island, dating back to the early eighteenth-century Huguenots. Having studied at Cordon Bleu, Claire is the inspiration behind the meticulously-prepared, four-course dinners. She makes liberal use of fresh island ingredients, including herbs, vegetables, and fruit grown right on the grounds. The "planter's-style" dinners include such specialties as pumpkin and coconut soup, warm chicken and mango salad, shrimps with paw paw and chili sauce, and guava-and-lime parfait.

Life at Rawlins has the sophisticated air of an English country house, complete with a grass tennis court, afternoon tea, and croquet. With no telephones or televisions in the rooms, there is nothing left to do but settle back on the veranda with a long, cool rum punch and absorb the soft, peaceful setting.

RAWLINS PLANTATION INN, P.O. Box 340, St. Kitts, West Indies; (809) 465-6221; Fax (809) 465-4954; Paul & Claire Rawson, owners. Represented by J.D.B. Associates at (800) 346-5358. Ten rooms, all with private baths. No air conditioning. High season rates: $250 to $375; low season: $175 to $255, including full English breakfast, afternoon tea, and dinner. No children under 13; smoking allowed; Visa/MasterCard/American Express. Spring-fed swimming pool on premises. Brimstone Hill Fortress, beaches, and rain forest trips nearby. Restaurant on premises, but few other restaurants nearby.

DIRECTIONS: on northwest St. Kitts, 45 minutes from the airport (about $25 by taxi). Hotel can arrange a taxi.

The pool area, high in the mountains.

LADERA RESORT

Room with a view

Talk about a room with a view! This is a place that has to be seen to be believed. A single row of suites and villas are perched at the edge of a thousand-foot cliff that hovers midway between St. Lucia's spectacular Pitons—a pair of volcanic peaks that rise vertically out of the sea. On top of that, the entire view-facing wall of each suite is missing—no window, no screen, nothing. It's a most bizarre sensation to feel so exposed to nature and dwarfed by such awesome scenery while sitting right in your room.

Even with the open wall, each suite is designed for maximum privacy, so no one but the birds can see you. Built of natural stone, tropical hardwood-paneled walls, brick floors, and cathedral ceilings, most of the suites feature individual plunge pools and sitting areas, plus four-poster canopied beds swathed in mosquito netting. Some showers are made of rock and open to the sun with skylights.

Left, Piton, a volcanic peak, seen from the bar's terrace.

The furnishings may be civilized, but the overall atmosphere is quite organic. Live plants grow right inside each room, and there is no barrier between you and the hillside foliage. Birds flutter freely in and out, serving as a constant reminder that it is not *they* who are indoors but rather *you* who are out-of-doors. It's a nature-lover's dream, but not for those who are overly squeamish about finding an occasional frog in their shower or insects in the room.

Also on the premises is a library with television and VCR, an open-air dining room called Dasheene, and an attractive swimming pool which was used in the filming of "Superman II." From the bar and pool terrace, you can sip on your welcome cocktail and contemplate this mesmerizing panorama.

LADERA RESORT, P.O. Box 225, Soufrière, St. Lucia, West Indies; (809) 459-7323; Fax (809) 459-5156; Frode Sund, manager. Represented by CARIBA! at (800) 841-4145. Nineteen open-air suites and villas, all with private baths; some with private pools. High season rates: $300 to $850; low season: $175 to $626, including tropical breakfast. Honeymoon and wedding packages available. Children welcome; smoking allowed; German, French, and Norwegian spoken; all credit cards accepted. Piton Mountains, Diamond Waterfalls, mineral baths, and rain forests nearby. Shuttle service to Soufrière and nearby beaches provided. Dasheene Restaurant recommended for dining.

DIRECTIONS: in southern St. Lucia, 40 minutes northeast of Hewanorra Airport. Complimentary airport transfers provided from Hewanorra, but not from Vigie Airport. Car rental not recommended.

Overleaf, one of the sensational suites overlooking the sea 1,000 feet below.

The lounge/library.

Sitting room of an oceanfront suite.

LA SAMANNA

Perfection— for a fortunate few

If you have to ask how much this place is, you probably can't afford it, but La Samanna certainly is one sybaritic bit of heaven. Situated on fifty-five secluded acres of Long Bay, in St. Martin, this sizable yet intimate hotel rates a ten for its tranquil, low-key luxury.

It begins right when you check in—not at the reception building but in the privacy of your own room. Within minutes a welcome fruit punch and exquisitely arranged fruit basket—complete with gold-trimmed kumquat leaves—is delivered to your door. One step off your balcony brings you directly onto the downy-soft sand, where the emerald blue sea sparkles invitingly through the palm trees. After a refreshing swim in the crystal clear water, you can dip your sandy feet in a huge conch shell filled with water. Your shower is accompanied by exotic, complimentary bottles of wonderfully-scented potions and white cotton yakuta robes.

Life at La Samanna seems designed solely to sooth the body and spirit. Nearly every door, window

LA SAMANNA, P.O. Box 477, 97064 St. Martin Cedex, French Antilles; (011) 590-876400; Fax (011) 590-878786; Ulrich Krauer, manager. Represented by Mary Ann DeNatteo at (800) 854-2252. Closed September and October. Seventy-eight rooms, all with private baths and air conditioning. High season rates: $490 to $1750; low season: $325 to $1400, including full breakfast; MAP plan available. Children welcome; smoking allowed; French, German and Spanish spoken; all credit cards accepted. Tennis courts, swimming pool, fitness center, movie room, and private beach on preimses. Mullet Bay casinos nearby. La Samanna, Fish Pot, and La Rosa recommended for dining.

DIRECTIONS: on Long Bay in southwest St. Martin (just over the Dutch border), 10 minutes from the airport (about $10 by taxi). Car rental recommended for exploring the island.

Left above, the pool and main building. Below, the beach at Baie Longue.

and balcony of the Moorish-inspired hotel is framed by a graceful archway, creating an exotic, sensual effect. The dazzling white of the guest building and sand is broken only by a clean contrast of blue trim, sea, and sky. The airy, white guest rooms are furnished in finely woven wicker and tasteful batik fabrics of subdued blue, coral, and green.

Each day begins with a scrumptious breakfast buffet on a dining terrace which opens to a stunning view of Long Bay. The only decision of the day is whether to lounge by the pool, have your "eleveneses" in the Moroccan-style bar, or take a walk on the sand, which is raked each morning into Zen-like patterns.

A colorful fruit basket welcomes you.
Overleaf, the panoramic dining terrace overlooking Baie Longue.

THE OYSTER POND BEACH HOTEL

Twin views of beach and marina

Oyster Pond commands not just one, but two, idyllic views. Jutting out on a narrow, rocky peninsula of eastern St. Maarten, this Moorish-designed hotel overlooks sailboat-filled Oyster Pond to the north and pristine Dawn Beach to the south.

Each of the five guest buildings are bright white with pink trim, castle-like roof lines, arched windows, and balconies. The main level of each building is landscaped with tropical flowers while a pretty double staircase curves up to the second floor. The rooms and suites are luxuriously stocked with amenities yet unpretentiously appointed with red tile floors and fresh, colorful fabrics against a clean background of white wicker and white walls. Each room has a wonderful arched balcony overlooking the blue-green sea and rocky coastline. If the mile-long crescent of Dawn Beach didn't look so inviting, one could spend all day on this balcony just basking in the cool breezes and soothing sound of the surf breaking on the rocks. A salt water swimming pool, surrounded by a narrow wood deck, also hangs over the ocean. From here, a short pathway leads to Dawn Beach.

The reception building is nicely appointed, with plenty of private nooks and conversation corners. The bar turns into a lively place during happy hour, especially when manager Jan Borsje is juggling drinks and jokes. If guests ever make it out to the dining room, they will be rewarded by a delicious menu of fresh seafood selections such as red snapper served in vermouth sauce. Upon returning to their rooms, they will find white terry robes draped on the beds, each decorated with a red hibiscus blossom.

Every balcony has a sensational ocean view.

THE OYSTER POND BEACH HOTEL, Oyster Bay, P.O. Box 239, St. Maarten, Netherlands Antilles; (800) 839-3030; (011) 599-522206; Fax (011) 599-525695; Jan Borsje, manager. Closed September 1 to October 8. Sixteen rooms and twenty-four suites, all with private baths and air conditioning. High season rates: $170 to $310; low season: $120 to $200, including breakfast. Inquire about children; smoking allowed; Dutch, French and Spanish spoken; Visa/MasterCard/American Express. Scuba diving, snorkeling, sailing, and casino excursions can be arranged. Yvette Restaurant, La Rosa, and Seafood Galley recommended for dining.

DIRECTIONS: on Oyster Bay, 5 miles from Philipsburg and 25 minutes from the airport (about $20 by taxi). Car rental recommended for exploring the island.

Left, above, the hotel seen from a private beach nearby. Below, The Oyster Pond, with its dock and anchorage.

The Osprey Suite.

The pool and dining terrace overlooks the harbor.

BLACKBEARD'S CASTLE

People come here for the view

The old stone tower that rises from the center of Blackbeard's Castle has long been a landmark on the hilltop above Charlotte Amalie. It was built in 1679 as a watchtower to scan the sea for pirates and enemy ships. Blackbeard himself was reputed to have used this tower as his hideaway. Since the contemporary hotel that surrounds it opened in 1985, the tower has remained largely unused.

The hotel commands a sensational view of the bustling, red-roofed town and its picturesque, boat-filled harbor—a steep, five-minute walk downhill and breathless, longer hike back up. From the panoramic bar, informal restaurant, and swimming pool you can watch the sleek cruise ships glide in and out of the island-dotted harbor. At this lofty height, guests are peacefully removed from the tourist bustle below.

The accommodations, though somewhat blandly decorated, are clean and comfortable, with air

Left above, Blackbeard's Tower and guest quarters. Below, a view of cruise ships in the harbor from the dining terrace.

conditioning, cable television, room safes, and telephones. Distributed among three buildings, some of the guest rooms, like the newly renovated junior suites, offer harbor views and patios enclosed with latticework, whereas the smaller bedrooms behind the restaurant have little balconies overlooking Charlotte Amalie.

But it's really the view that draws visitors here. At sunset, you'll find guests out on the terrace enjoying aptly-named concoctions such as the "pirate's revenge." In the evenings, live jazz is offered in the dining room, which is also a favorite spot for Sunday brunches.

The pleasant staff, reasonable rates, and unbeatable view make Blackbeard's Castle a good choice for those who wish to be within walking distance of Charlotte Amalie but not right in it.

BLACKBEARD'S CASTLE, Blackbeard's Hill, P.O. Box 6041, St. Thomas, U.S. Virgin Islands 00804-6041 (800) 344-5771; (809) 776-1234; Fax (809) 776-4321; Bob Harrington & Henrique Konzen, owners. Open all year. Eighteen rooms and six suites, all with private baths and air conditioning. High season rates: $110 to $190; low season: $75 to $145, including continental breakfast. Inquire about children; smoking allowed; French, Portuguese, Spanish and German spoken; all credit cards accepted. Swimming pool on premises. Beaches, tennis, golf, sailing, and duty-free shopping nearby. Blackbeard's Castle recommended for dining.

DIRECTIONS: on Government Hill, in Charlotte Amalie, 20 minutes from the airport (about $5 per person by taxi). Car rental not necessary.

Overleaf, the stunning view of the harbor and town of Charlotte Amalie from the castle's dining terrace.

The entry.

HOTEL 1829

Rustic, romantic guest rooms

Hotel 1829 is conveniently close to the thriving center of Charlotte Amalie—the busiest cruise ship port in the Caribbean. Set on Government Hill, a short walk up from the main shopping district, this terraced hotel is steeped in a multinational history. Built in 1829 by a French sea captain for his bride, the structure was designed by an Italian architect in a Spanish motif and completed with African and Danish labor. Elevated just high enough to take in a view of the town and harbor, the hotel is randomly constructed on different levels with maze-like steps winding steeply from room to room. Its Old World, melon-colored façade, white trim, potted palms, and green awnings add to the rich, textural effect.

Though the guest rooms vary in size, they all exude a rustic, romantic mood, with old brick walls, red tile floors, tall wooden shutters, paddle fans, and four-poster wicker beds draped with mosquito

Left, the hotel and pool and harbor view.

netting. Add to this such modern-day comforts as cable televisions, telephones, air conditioning, and mini-refrigerators. Some suites, like Number One, are particularly spacious, with a separate sitting area and miniature balcony.

Halfway up the hill is a small swimming pool where guests can cool off after a hot day of shopping or sightseeing. But the focal point here is the pub-style bar which has been built into the old Danish kitchen. With its rough stone walls, two-hundred-year-old Moroccan tiled floors, and aging hearth still visible, the pub has a dark, cool, inviting look. The adjoining dining room, which is also quite atmospheric, opens onto a veranda where a continental breakfast is enjoyed each morning. From here, one can watch the crowds of cruise ship passengers swarming into the duty-free shops and narrow alleyways that beg to be explored.

HOTEL 1829, 30 Kongens Gade, P.O. Box 1567, St. Thomas, U.S. Virgin Islands 00804; (800) 524-2002; (809) 776-1829; Fax (809) 776-4313; Baron Vernon Ball & Michael Ball, owners. Open all year. Thirteen rooms and two suites, all with private baths and air conditioning. High season rates: $70 to $280, low season: $50 to $190, including continental breakfast. No children under 12; smoking allowed; all credit cards accepted. Coral World, Mountain Top, Drakes Seat, and Magens Bay nearby. Cuzzins, Victors Hide Out, and Zorba's recommended for dining.

DIRECTIONS: in Charlotte Amalie, 20 minutes from the airport (about $5 per person by taxi). Car rental not necessary.

Room 1 in evening light.

COBBLESTONE INN

A cozy, overnight stopping place

Though Kingstown itself is not a big tourist destina-tion, the bustling old harbor serves as a major port and gateway to the Grenadines. From here you can ferry or fly to Bequia, Mustique, or the more remote islands of Canouan, Union Island, and Mayreau. And once outside of Kingstown, the volcano-capped island of St. Vincent is filled with lush, tranquil beauty.

The Cobblestone Inn is the coziest place to stay for those overnighting in Kingstown. Built in 1814 as a sugar warehouse (and later for arrowroot, of which St. Vincent produces most of the world's supply), this historic inn is in the waterfront district, just a few blocks from the ferry terminal. Its Georgian-style exterior is distinguished by old stone walls, white grillwork, and periwinkle blue trim. Set back from the busy street by a cobblestone passageway, the inn begins on the second level where a cheery reception-television lounge and the most desirable guest rooms are found. Then it runs in a labyrinth-like fashion up to the third floor where there is an open-air dining room and smaller guest rooms. While not overly fancy, the bedrooms are all functional, clean, and air conditioned.

The Cobblestone Inn also draws a loyal following of businesspeople looking for a convenient in-town lodging. In the evenings most of them hang out downstairs in an inviting, British-style pub called Basil's Bar.

Guest quarters.

The stonework of the building gave the inn its name.

COBBLESTONE INN, P.O. Box 867, Bay Street, Kingstown, St. Vincent and the Grenadines, West Indies; (809) 456-1937; Fax (809) 456-1938; Ann Joshua, owner. Open all year. Nineteen rooms, all with private baths and air conditioning. Year-round rates: $54, single; $71, double, including continental breakfast. Children under 12 free; smoking allowed; all credit cards accepted. Sightseeing and snorkeling tours can be arranged. Basil's Bar, Vee Jay's Rooftop Diner, Sid's Pub, and French Restaurant recommended for dining.

DIRECTIONS: in central Kingstown, 4 miles from the airport (about $8 by taxi). Car rental optional.

The main building, set in the jungle.

Exotic orchids grow freely on the grounds.

ARNOS VALE HOTEL

Heaven—especially for bird watchers

It comes as no surprise that this intimate resort is Italian-owned, because this dreamy stretch of Tobago (pronounced "Toe-BAY-go") coastline does somewhat resemble a tropical version of the Italian Riviera. Over sixty acres of thick vegetation and exotic flowers tumble down the slopes into a bowl-like valley. At its base is a sandy cove which hides a fantastic reef of coral and some of the best snorkeling in the southern Caribbean. Once an old estate, Arnos Vale itself has the Old World look of a European lodge.

A wide array of accommodations are scattered over the hillside. The main reception building is highlighted by a bar and dining room of heavily-beamed ceilings. Up the hill, another guest building contains bedrooms that are tastefully appointed with light floral fabrics, warm wood, and wicker. Higher still are several small cottages. At the bottom of the slope, by the swimming pool, are two newer guest buildings, some containing attractive oceanfront suites.

No matter where you stay you'll get lots of exercise trekking up and down these hills. But the lushly landscaped pathways that sweep over the grounds make walking a pleasure. Every exotic flower imaginable is in bloom. Not to be missed is the gently forested walk to Sunset Point, a panoramic lookout where you can view the verdant coastal countryside from two stragically-placed chairs.

For bird lovers, Arnos Vale is a veritable haven. The terraced bar, which hovers a hundred feet above the sea, is a great place to settle down for some serious bird watching. Every evening a staff member lures the birds out of the flamboyant trees with tasty slices of fresh mango. Some of the mot-mots, bananaquits, and wild parrots are so tame they'll eat right out of your hand.

This is the kind of place where you could easily spend a week snorkeling, hiking, and communing quietly with nature in blissful, secluded comfort.

ARNOS VALE HOTEL, P.O. Box 208, Scarborough, Tobago, West Indies; (809) 639-2881; Fax (809) 639-4629; Vittorio de Felice, manager. Closed October 1 to December 15. Twenty-six rooms and three suites, all with private baths and air conditioning. High season rates: $110 per person; low season: $85 per person, including breakfast. Children welcome; smoking allowed; Italian spoken; Visa/MasterCard/American Express. Gemma's by the Sea, Black Rock Cafe, and Old Donkey Cart House recommended for dining.

DIRECTIONS: on Arnos Vale Road, just outside of Plymouth, 7 miles from the airport (about $10 by taxi). Car rental recommended.

Room 5.

Right, bird watching is a major attraction at the inn.

Sitting on the terrace brings you close to nature.

RICHMOND GREAT HOUSE INN

Renowned for its African art

While swinging from a hammock of the Richmond Great House, it's easy to imagine what life might have been like for a planter; perhaps because this eighteenth-century estate is utterly isolated from the present-day world. Here on the southern coast of Tobago, you won't find many reminders of twentieth-century life—not even a gas station. The verdant landscape sprawls unbroken before the inn much the same as it was in the colonial days.

Once part of a cocoa and coconut estate, the great house has an authentic West Indian feel, with its airy cathedral ceilings, wood floors, paddle fans, and abundance of tall picture windows opening to ethereal vistas of the rolling countryside. The main hall is occupied by a dining room, and emanating from this are five simply-decorated guest rooms of varying sizes, plus a library filled to the brim with books. New guest rooms—each with their own private patios—have recently been added to the

Left, the dining room and lounge beyond show off part of the African art collection.

The Great House from the pool.

lower level. Though smaller and with less character than the great house rooms, they are fresh looking and naturally cooled by the ocean breezes.

What really sets this inn apart is that it contains the largest private collection of African art and artifacts in the Caribbean. The Tobago-born owner, Dr. Hollis R. Lynch, is a professor of African History at Columbia University, and he has spent a lifetime collecting the many treasures found throughout the common rooms—Kenté cloth hangings, instruments, wood carvings, chests, masks, combs, and furnishings from Ghana, Nigeria, Tanzania and Zaire. They lend a wonderfully exotic air to the old house. When "the professor" (as his staff calls him) is in residence, his wealth of knowledge is equally fascinating. His inn is more than just a B&B—it's a civilized piece of history.

RICHMOND GREAT HOUSE INN, Belle Garden, Tobago, Trinidad and Tobago, West Indies; (809) 660-4467; Fax (809) 660-4467; Vernon George, manager. Open all year. Ten rooms and suites, all with private baths. No air conditioning. High season rates: $80 to $160; low season: $75 to $145, including full breakfast; MAP plan available. No children under 10; smoking allowed; Visa accepted. Bird watching, swimming pool, tennis court, activities center, badminton, and croquet on premises. Beach nearby. Day tours and group facilities available. Richmond Great House recommended for dining. Nearest restaurants (Gemma's and Blue Waters Inn) are 45 minutes away.

DIRECTIONS: on southern Tobago, 45 minutes from the airport. Free airport transportation and car rentals can be arranged by the inn.

One of the items in the African art collection.

A colorful guest room.

The Gazebo Bar has a view of the water.

SUGAR MILL HOTEL

Hosts with a passion for food

The Sugar Mill is equally, if not more, acclaimed for its cuisine than for its accommodations. It's no wonder, considering that proprietors Jeff and Jinx Morgan—both seasoned cookbook writers and long-time columnists for *Bon Appétit*—have an obvious passion for food. Blending their culinary skills, San Francisco background, and the West Indian flavors of Tortola together, they have created one of the finest dining experiences on the island.

The restaurant is also the most atmospheric part of the Sugar Mill. Once the old boiling house of a seventeenth-century sugar plantation, its walls are built of thick stone formerly used as ballast on cargo ships, with cornerstones of brain and star coral. Glowing candles and high raftered ceilings turn this room into a romantic scene at night.

Adjoining this is an open-air bar, breakfast room, and pretty pavilion which form the centerpiece of the hotel. Up the nicely-landscaped slope is a round swimming pool which is built directly over the site of the old oxen treadmill. Above this are a variety of comfortable guest rooms, suites and villas, all with private balconies and most with kitchenettes. While most of the rooms feature standard hotel décor, the two-bedroom villa—where the Morgans resided until recently—is quite luxurious and colorful, with a full living area, kitchen, and long balcony opening to stunning views of Apple Bay.

Left above, the pool area and tropical foliage. Below, The hotel beach and Islands Restaurant.

The dining room is housed in an original stone building on the grounds of the plantation.

Across the street is a casual oceanfront café where the lunches are also exceptional. While a small beach and sunning terrace adjoin the café, the glistening, mile-long beach at Long Bay is just a short jaunt down the road.

Things are extremely well-run here, due in no small part to the Morgans' attentive British-American staff. New arrivals will find helpful island information kits in their rooms and complimentary welcome drinks in the gazebo.

SUGAR MILL HOTEL, P.O. Box 425, Road Town, Tortola, British Virgin Islands; (809) 495-4355; Fax (809) 495-4696; Jeff & Jinx Morgan, owners; Patrick Conway, manager. Represented by C.I.L. at (800) 633-7411. Closed August and September. Twenty-one rooms, suites and villas, all with private baths. Air conditioning in delux villa. High season rates: $170 to $250; low season: $130 to $175, with breakfast available at an extra charge; MAP plan available. Children under 10 not allowed during high season; smoking allowed; Spanish, German, and French spoken; Visa/MasterCard/American Express. Beach and swimming pool on premises. Sugar Mill Restaurant, Islands Restaurant, and Brandywine Bay recommended for dining. Try a drink at Bomba's Shack.

DIRECTIONS: on western Tortola, 45 minutes from the airport (about $24 by taxi), and 20 minutes from Road Town. Car rental recommended for exploring the island.

Owners Fred and Barbara Zollna.

ZOLLNA HOUSE

Accomodating hosts who love Trinidad

Trinidad is perhaps best known for its Carnival—a wild, five-night revelry held every year before Lent. The Zollna House offers a quiet, more affordable retreat from the big hotels that are right in the party zone. Located just two miles from Port of Spain in the residential foothills of the Maraval Valley, this B&B actually consists of two modern homes that are just a block apart. Both are highlighted by terraces that overlook the distant city and Gulf of Paria. The guest rooms are clean and Scandinavian-like in their simplicity, with island art work, wood carvings, and fresh-cut tropical flowers spicing up the otherwise functional décor. Common areas include a living room and cheerful breakfast room in the main house.

The Zollna House is run by Fred Zollna—a German-born, U.S.-raised, thirty-year resident of Trinidad—and Barbara, his Trinidad-born wife of Chinese-Spanish descent. An extremely accommodating couple, they bend over backwards to make sure their guests are taken care of. Through Fred

Room 7.

Ginger grows in the garden.

ZOLLNA HOUSE, 12 Ramlogan Development, P.O. Box 624, Maraval, Port of Spain, Trinidad and Tobago; (809) 628-3731; Fax (809) 627-0856; Gottfried F. Zollna, owner. Open all year. Twelve rooms in two houses, some with shared baths. No air conditioning. Carnival rates (5-night minimum): $40 to $71; rest-of-the-year rates: $30 to $70, including full breakfast. Children over 7 welcome; smoking allowed in designated areas; German spoken; Visa/MasterCard/American Express. Sailing, fishing, and nature excursions available. Ali Baba, China Palace, and Gourmet Club recommended for dining. No restaurants within walking distance.

DIRECTIONS: in the Maraval Valley, near Port of Spain, 20 miles from the airport. Pickup available upon request. Car rental can be arranged through Zollna House.

Left, the front exterior of the house.

and Barbara, guests will discover that there is more to Trinidad than just its Carnival. Once outside of the city, the island is a lush, unspoiled nature-lover's paradise. The Zollnas love it so much that they are currently building a small hotel on the remote north coast, about an hour away. Surrounded by a national forest, this resort will have its own restaurant, secluded beach (right where the leatherback turtles lay their eggs in the sand), rain forest trails, and fresh-water swimming lagoon. When it is completed, The Zollnas will be able to offer guests the best of both worlds—the cultural excitement of Port of Spain and the natural wonders of Trinidad.

Owners Carol and Charlie, with dogs Rusty and Timmy.

The guest quarters.

Room 14.

OLDE YARD INN

Four acres of rolling lawns and tropical gardens

The Olde Yard Inn enjoys a peaceful setting in the Virgin Gorda Valley amid four acres of rolling lawns and tropically landscaped gardens. This friendly, family-run inn attracts visitors who want to hike, dive, and swim on Virgin Gorda yet don't want to stay at a fancy resort.

The inn's airy dining room and bar serve as both the reception area—where owner Carol Kaufman greets all her guests personally—and one of the most popular restaurants on the island. Not only is it nicely appointed, with high cedar ceilings, Virgin Islands artwork, and classical music playing, but the food is outstanding. Carol's husband Charlie is also the chef here, and he lovingly prepares all of the pastas, soups, breads, dressings, and desserts from scratch. Everything, from the swordfish to the key lime pie, literally melts in your mouth.

Adjacent to the dining room is a two-story block of guest rooms, most with their own private balconies. The small, immaculate, wicker-furnished bedrooms are warmed by mauve-colored spreads and cedar paneling, yet cooled by the Atlantic breezes wafting through the jalousie windows.

Left, the Library, the center of activity.

A big draw here is the library, which boasts one of the biggest hotel book collections in the Caribbean. Two adjoining octagonal pavilions are lined with thousands of books and cushioned reading chairs, while a piano, television, and videos offer additional entertainment. Carol and Charlie claim that some guests disappear in there and never come out.

The entire inn is built with lounging and reading in mind. With only the sounds of the wind chimes and the occasional rooster, there is nothing to disturb one's sense of tranquility here.

OLDE YARD INN, P.O. Box 26, Virgin Gorda, British Virgin Islands; (809) 495-5544; Fax (809) 495-5986; Carol Kaufman-Williams, owner. Represented by Caribbean Inns Ltd. at (800) 633-7411. Open all year. Fourteen rooms, all with private baths. Air conditioning in four rooms. High season rates: $125 to $170; low season: $75 to $95, with breakfast available for $3.50 to $10. MAP plans and honeymoon packages available. Children welcome; smoking allowed; Visa/MasterCharge/American Express. Swimming pool, Jacuzzi and exercise room currently underway. Beach one mile away. The Baths, The Coppermine, and Gorda Peak nearby. Olde Yard Inn, Little Dix Bay, and Biras Creek recommended for dining.

DIRECTIONS: five minutes from the airport and ferry dock. Car rental recommended for exploring the island.

CARIBBEAN B&B AGENCIES

CAPTAIN'S QUARTERS SALES OFFICE. (212) 289-6031; Fax (212) 289-1931. Represents Saba.

CARIBA! 313 North Tioga Street, Ithaca, NY 14850; (800) 841-4145; Fax (607) 273-5302. Open 9 to 5 Monday to Friday. Represents St. Lucia, Bequia.

CARIBBEAN INNS LTD. P.O. Box 7411, Hilton Head, SC 19938; (800) 633-7411; Fax (803) 686-7411. Open 9 to 5:30, Monday to Friday; 10 to 12 noon Saturday. Represents most islands.

E & M ASSOCIATES. 211 East 43rd Street, New York City, NY 10017; (212) 599-8280; Fax (212) 599-1755. Open 9 to 6 Monday to Friday. Represents Antigua, Nevis, Bequia.

INTERNATIONAL HOTEL REPRESENTATIVES (IHR). 2200 Fletcher Avenue, 9W Office Center, Fort Lee, NJ 07024; (800) 346-7084; Fax (201) 346-0511. Open 9 to 5, Monday to Friday. Represents Anguilla, Aruba, and Jamaica.

INTERNATIONAL TRAVEL RESORTS (ITR). 4 Park Avenue, New York City, NY 10016; (212) 251-1800; Fax (212) 251-1767. Open 8:30 to 7, Monday to Friday; 9 to 4:30 Saturday. Represents most islands.

J.D.B. ASSOCIATES. P.O. Box 16086, Alexandria, VA 22302-6086; (800) 346-5358; Fax (703) 548-5825. Open 9 to 5:30 Monday to Friday. Represents St. Lucia, St. John, St. Barts, St. Kitts, Nevis, Jamaica, Peter Island.

RALPH LOCKE ISLANDS, INC. P.O. Box 492477, Los Angeles, CA 90049-8477; (800) 223-1108; (310) 440-4220. Open 6 to 5 Monday to Friday. Represents Aruba, Barbados, Grenada, St. Barts, St. Croix, St. Lucia, St. Vincent, Mustique, Virgin Gorda.

RAY MORROW ASSOCIATES. 4228 Hermitage Road, Virginia Beach, VA 23455; (800) 243-9420. Open 9 to 6 Monday to Friday. Represents Jamaica.

ROBERT REID ASSOCIATES. 810 North 96th Street, Omaha, NE 68114-2594; (800) 223-6510; Fax (402) 398-5484. Open 8 A.M. to 8 P.M. Monday to Friday; 9 to 3 Saturday. Represents most islands.